*What the experts say about T*
**Storytelling**

"Peter Rubie's book, a model of sound advice and insight, will benefit writers, newcomers, and professionals alike."
*—Richard Curtis, literary agent and author of*
Beyond the Bestseller

"Peter Rubie's emphasis on becoming a storyteller is exactly what beginning writers need to hear to master the difficult craft of writing fiction. I unreservedly recommend this book to all aspiring novelists."
*—Kent Carroll, Publisher and Executive Editor,*
*Carroll & Graf Publishers*

"I wish I'd had *The Elements of Storytelling* when I taught writing on the college level. It is a wonderful read as well as a provocative workbook. The exercises Peter Rubie suggests are at first glance sheer fun—at second glance much, much more."
*—Elise Donner, Executive Editor, Kensington Publishing*

"This invaluable step-by-step guide should be on every writer's bookshelf right between *The Elements of Style* and the thesaurus."
*—Tom Colgan, Senior Editor, Avon Books*

"Rubie has an intimate and practical understanding of fiction writing. Reading this book is akin to having a perceptive teacher peer over your shoulder as you work and provide thoughtful guidance."
*—Kate Stine, Editor in Chief, Otto Penzler Books*

"If you read this book closely and carefully, your writing cannot help but be vastly improved."
*—Albert Zuckerman, President, Writers House, Inc., Literary*
*Agency, and author of* Writing the Blockbuster Novel

"Peter Rubie has written a wonderful book that every aspiring professional writer should own."
　　　　—*Matthew Bialer, literary agent, William Morris Agency*

"Every fiction writer needs this book, either to learn the essential principle of effective writing or to remind oneself of what it is that makes fiction compelling."
　　　　—*J. Madison David, novelist and Senior Professor, Professional Writing Program, University of Oklahoma*

"If you really want to understand how to create stories that will sell in today's market, you could buy a book by a writer, another by an editor, and a third by a literary agent. But it would be smarter to buy *The Elements of Storytelling* by writer-editor-agent Peter Rubie. Rubie explains the secrets of creating drama though the written word. His vast knowledge is clear, honest, and helpful."
　　　　—*Gary Provost, novelist, author, and teacher*

"Peter Rubie sets down *The Elements of Storytelling* with a clarity and panache that make it *de rigueur* for writers. This book will make you laugh, it will make you think, and, best of all, it will make you a better writer."
　　　　—*Lynn Hightower, author of* Satan's Lambs, Shamus Award for Best First Novel

"*The Elements of Storytelling* delivers what it promises and is a book I wish I'd read before taking up fiction writing, because it would have taught me lots of things—entertainingly and economically—that I learnt by hard trial and frequent error instead. I would not hesitate to recommend it to aspiring writers, or to better published ones who need reminding of the essentials of the craft. (That's all of us, by the way!)"
　　　　—*Robert Goddard, bestselling author of* In Pale Battalions *and* Full Circle

# The Elements
# of Storytelling

# The Elements of Storytelling

## How to Write Compelling Fiction

Peter Rubie

John Wiley & Sons, Inc.
New York • Chichester • Brisbane • Toronto • Singapore

Copyright © 1996 by Peter Rubie
Published by John Wiley & Sons, Inc.

ISBN 0-471-13045-1

Printed in the United States of America

10  9  8  7  6  5  4  3  2  1

To my good friend, agent, and partner, Lori Perkins—and to all the writers, published and unpublished, with whom I have come in contact over the years, in particular John, Lynn, Beth, Sid, Jim Cohen, Jim Davis, Vince, Gary, and Carol. It is through your talent and imaginations that I have learned the little I know so far about editing and writing well.

# Acknowledgments

I would like to thank my editor, PJ Dempsey, and her assistant, Chris Jackson, and copyeditor Louann Werksma, whose suggestions made this a better book; and Sylvia K. Burack, without whose initial encouragement this book would have been stillborn.

# Contents

# Introduction

"I wouldn't say I was in the 'great' class, but I had a great time while I was trying to be great."

*—Harry S Truman*

*The Elements of Storytelling for Writers* aims to give fiction writers the basic tools needed to write a story and a map to help them avoid the obstacles that lie in the path of the unwary storyteller.

It differs from other writing manuals in that it offers a holistic approach to storytelling. By *holistic* I mean a continual emphasis on the overview of your work. While it's necessary to teach storytelling as a series of related topics, it's important for the student to keep in mind that these components are both interconnected and interdependent.

## 1. The Two Basic Elements

The components of fiction, such as dialogue, voice, description, and so on are dictated by and stem from two basic elements: plot and character.

1

Stories, in essence, are about what characters do next, and why. The art of the storyteller is figuring out a story. The craft of the storyteller is working out the best way to tell that story. Storytelling, while essentially simple, is, paradoxically, difficult to master: You come up with a plot and then invent dynamic characters who move through that plot, weaving the story from the conflicts and dramas of their lives.

If writers aren't careful, and they focus on one component of fiction at the expense of another (e.g., dialogue over description), their approach to storytelling may be similar to that of the blind men who examined the elephant, one feeling the tail, another the trunk, a third the leg, all claiming the elephant to be something other than it is.

## 2.   *What Will Happen When I Get Published?*

Many writers have unrealistic expectations of what will happen after they achieve their goal of getting into print for the first time, so it's worthwhile asking, "How do I imagine my life will change once my story is published?"

Money? Well, you'll get some compensation certainly, but unless you're very lucky you won't make enough money writing fiction to do it exclusively, at least at first; so you'll more than likely have to do something else to pay the bills.

Fame? Andy Warhol reckoned everybody gets fifteen minutes of fame, and while I sincerely hope you get yours, few of us become household names like Dean Koontz, Stephen King, Mary Higgins Clark, or Louis L'Amour. While there are some 50,000 books published annually in the United States alone, this figure is shrinking; and it's not getting any easier for first novelists to get their fiction published. There's no guarantee that, having been published once, you will be published again. Each work is judged on its own merits, and some writers only have one book in them.

## 3.  Talent

The concept of talent is vague and much abused. Either God's hand has touched you or it hasn't, but whatever blessing you were born with is only a seed. To bloom, it needs the careful nurturing of your sweat, dedication, and intelligence. I have known many talented people who never amounted to much because they weren't prepared to apply themselves. At first, it was all too easy and their gift never meant that much to them. Once they realized that to survive in the arts they'd have to do the same sustained hard work as all those other "less talented" people, most gave up.

Talent, in large part, can be defined as the speed it takes someone to learn something. The faster you absorb information, the more talented you probably are. Talent also involves the ability to imaginatively use that acquired knowledge. It has very litle to do with how old you are.

The greater your native talent, however, the greater your *responsibility* not to waste it. Whether or not you have a talent for writing is something only you can decide for yourself. The mere *desire* to write has no more worth or meaning than does the desire to be rich, healthy, and happy. Writing (or playing music, or learning to be a gymnast or whatever your calling happens to be) is a compulsion. An author friend once told me, only partly in jest, "If I ever find the bitch who made me like this, I'll kill her." I know exactly how she feels. Most writers hate writing, but can't stop themselves from doing it.

## 4.  Learning the Rules

One thing is sure: If you practice writing long enough, and learn your craft well enough, you *will* eventually get published. When that finally happens, you feel an overwhelming pride in your achievement. You realize that all those years of study, rejection, hard work, and belief in yourself (often in the face of bitter discouragement) have been vindicated; and you learn that the work is ultimately its own reward.

In the beginning, writers of fiction look for rules about what they should and shouldn't do. That's probably one reason you bought this book. Eventually you learn there are no rules except the ones you make up. After all, art created by pre-scribed, rigid rules quickly ceases to be art and becomes propaganda. The very nature of art is invention.

There *are*, however, some general principles you should learn that will point you in the right direction. If the mechanics or techniques of writing can be compared with carpentry, then storytelling is akin to cabinetmaking. Anyone can learn to join a few pieces of wood, but not everyone can turn out a Chippendale chair or a Stradivarius violin.

## 5. Handling Rejection

If you've been writing and submitting material and you're still not yet published, you're probably doing something wrong. However obtuse you think editors are when they reject your brilliant piece, they aren't rejecting you out of spite. There is nothing more satisfying for an editor than to find a manu-script that's well presented, well written, and well thought out.

Because of my experiences as an agent, an editor, *and* a writer, I know all about rejection and the emotional turbulence that can sometimes accompany the author/editor, author/agent relationships. There is nothing more humbling or difficult to handle than learning that someone thinks what you wrote isn't up to scratch. Sometimes they're wrong and just don't "get it," but that doesn't happen often.

It's a brutal fact to face, but if something you've written is rejected consistently, more than likely it's because it just isn't good enough.  As an agent, I reject material primarily for that reason.

If that fact is true—and ninety-nine times out of one hundred it is—therein also lies your salvation. You hold the solution in your own hands.  Think things through more carefully, obey the rules you either did not know or thought you could ignore, and do the piece again.

Here are two rules of thumb to start you off.  Post them where you can see them whenever you sit down to write.

1.  Keep it simple, and

2.  If I'm still unpublished, I'm not yet the best judge of my work. I must go back to basics.

The basics are what this book is all about.

# Part One

## Techniques of Storytelling

# Learning the "Rules" of Storytelling: The Synopsis, Part 1

"A synopsis is a cold thing. You do it with the front of your mind. If you're going to stay with it, you never get quite the same magic as when you're going all out."

*–J. B. Priestley*

The value of any work of art owes much to the character and personality of the artist who created it. You need to learn the rules of writing fiction, not so that you can use them as formulae or crutches to produce safe, workmanlike stories, but so that mastering the craft of storytelling will liberate you from those rules.

There is a difference between freedom and license. Invention, the heart of storytelling, is the spontaneous generation of new rules. It derives from the *artistic freedom* that results when the writer masters basic technique and moves beyond it. The work of the artist Pablo Picasso, for example, whose draftsmanship at age fourteen is stunning, is a classic example of how a mastery of one's craft leads to the freedom of transcendent creativity. The same can also be said of the work of James Joyce who, toward the end of his life, said that all stories should begin, "Once upon a time." He actually managed to begin *A Portrait of the Artist as a Young Man* exactly that way.

License, on the other hand, is mistaken for creative freedom by the intellectually and artistically lazy who indulge in an egotistical pursuit of fame and fortune while avoiding the hard work needed to achieve them.

Thomas Mann once said, "A writer is somebody for whom writing is more difficult than it is for other people." Truman Capote later contributed, "When God hands you a gift, he also hands you a whip; and the whip is intended for self-flagellation solely."

## 1.1 How to Be Original

The mistake some unpublished writers make is believing that, to be original, one must reject or reinvent *all* the rules of storytelling without first fully understanding the purpose of those rules. In fact, with each story, a storyteller creates his or her own rules. The rules of writing discussed in this book are intended to be diagnostic instruments to help you create a story or fix one that isn't working.

A story must be judged by its own rules. If it fails, it is because either it follows no rules or the rules it follows are flawed. An example of this is when an idea or event is introduced that ought to affect the direction of the story, but it is subsequently either ignored or forgotten by the writer. The storyteller must always complete the equation—that is, think through the implications of what is happening in the story, not only in terms of character and action but also the form the piece of fiction has taken.

For example, if a novel, written in the form of a diary, describes a murder committed by the diarist at the beginning of the story, it is natural to suppose that the murder will play some part in the story that follows. If it doesn't, we ask ourselves, first, why bother to mention the murder in the first place? Second, we think the murderer is not convincing because such an act *must* have some sort of resonance to make him or her believable. (Even the *deliberate absence* of conscience or guilt over the act of murder is a form of resonance.)

If the diarist also gives us the thoughts of another character, without previously explaining that the character told the diarist what he was thinking at that moment, we are struck by the absurdity of one individual's being able to explicitly and accurately say what another is thinking. It is, moreover, a breach of the diary form of storytelling, because that form precludes going into the thoughts of another character. The diarist can tell us he *supposes* or *presumes* something that another was thinking, but that is not the same thing as knowing. An exception, of course, is if we establish early on that the diarist has some sort of psychic ability. Because it is such an outlandish element, however, that ability would need to play a major role in the story (other than merely serving as a device for going into another's thoughts) for its use to be justified.

A story's main function is to explore human emotions, values, and beliefs. Characters must come to know themselves in convincing situations and reveal that knowledge to the reader.

A story consists of a protagonist who has a goal (nearly always a recognizably human character—Richard Adams's *Watership Down* and Tolkien's *Lord of the Rings* are interesting variations on this) and an antagonist (not necessarily always human—take, for example, the big fish in *The Old Man and the Sea*, or the white whale in *Moby Dick*) whose function is to prevent the protagonist from achieving that goal. The conclusion of the story is the solution the protagonist devises to defeat or outwit the antagonist and attain his or her goal. At the very minimum, your *synopsis*, or story summary, should broadly cover these points.

In *The Hero with a Thousand Faces* (a book every writer of fiction should read), Joseph Campbell wrote, "A hero ventures forth from the world of common day into a region of supernatural wonder: fabulous forces are there encountered and a decisive victory is won: the hero comes back from this mysterious adventure with the power to bestow boons on his fellow man." While he was discussing myth and archetype, nevertheless, Campbell, I think, managed in one sentence to sum up the essential elements of a good story.

Here's an example of what I mean: A girl (our hero/heroine) born in the ghettos of Newark, New Jersey, and who has never been away from her immediate neighborhood, "ventures forth" into a region of—to her—"supernatural wonder," the skyscrapers of Manhattan island, whose spires and rooftops she can see from across the river every day, and whose riches and empowering qualities she constantly yearns for. Because of a bad home situation, she has run away. Now, settled in a poor section of Manhattan, surrounded by others who have similar heartbreaking stories and dreams of "making it" but no means to achieve their goals, the girl comes to realize that knowledge, not money, is real power, for knowledge can bring money. As a result, she determines to become as highly educated as she can. But "fabulous forces"—crushing poverty, difficulty in getting accepted in evening classes, working at a dispiriting job, sexual harassment, racial discrimination, and so on—conspire to defeat her. She eventually manages to get to college ("wins a decisive victory"), however, and returns to her neighborhood a teacher, driven to help and inspire others to better themselves and their neighborhood ("returning with the power to bestow boons on her fellows").

## 1.2    Three Steps to a Successful Story

All successful stories follow a broad pattern, outlined below. While the steps given are simplistic, they're not meant to be a template to write by but rather a checklist of a story's dramatic movement and dynamics. If your story deviates substantially from the following steps, you probably need to rethink it.

1. Introduce the protagonist, establish the status quo, and start the story at the dramatic point at which the status quo is about to end. The protagonist discovers he has a serious problem he must solve or pay a terrible price for his inaction.

2. In trying to solve the problem, the protagonist reveals his flaws and/or virtues, causing matters to become worse. He discovers a potential solution to his problem and starts to achieve that solution, only to find he has plunged himself (or someone he cares for) into even deeper trouble until things look hopeless.

3. Eventually, changed by his adventure, the protagonist solves the problem, in the process learning something about himself and/or something about the human condition of which he was previously ignorant. This new knowledge can point to the solution of the problem, or it can be the reward for solving the problem.

You'll notice that these three steps are not that different from Campbell's definition of the hero's journey. You might also try imposing this structure on some novels you've recently read. You'll find it fits the work of Charles Dickens, Leo Tolstoy, and Margaret Mitchell as comfortably as that of Joyce Carol Oates, Stephen King, and Danielle Steele. The reason, of course, is that, to be successful, good storytelling has an archetypal or "everyman" function.

## 1.3   The Story Is Not about What Happens, but to Whom It Happens

It is amazing how many manuscripts by weak writers do not have a main character, or sometimes any character, for the first ten or more pages. James Michener might be able to get away with it on occasion, but frankly he is the exception. Readers crave a human point of reference, someone to love or hate. *The story is not about what happens, but the character to whom it happens.* We are all instinctive storytellers—it is a natural human tendency—from telling jokes that are in effect abbreviated short stories to the anecdote you tell about the day's most interesting event when you get home at night. The novelist and short story writer must develop and refine that instinct for oral storytelling by learning how to commit it to paper.

One way to do this is to use the "man in a bar" technique. Imagine you're in a bar, and you're telling a story to the person sitting next to you. How would you tell it? I'd bet a pound to a penny that instead of beginning, "It was a dark and stormy night, and the wind was howling through the trees . . .," you'd more likely start off, "So this guy sees this ad for an exterminator and he thinks, 'I can do that.' He needs the money pretty bad, and even though the job means he has to go underground and work in the damp darkness killing rats the size of Pekingese . . . " Get the idea?

Here's an example of a story idea:

A young woman sacrifices her future to a brute to save her father from a terrible fate and, as a result, discovers her mate and finds happiness.

We already have three characters who seem to spring from the story idea—the brute, the young woman, and the father—so we're doing well so far. We've also given the father a problem to solve—his terrible fate, whatever that turns out to be—while the young woman's immediate problem is to decide whether to act selfishly and condemn her father, or betray herself and her dreams and hopes and save her father. And who is the brute? What is his story?

Interestingly, even at this stage, *who the characters are* largely determines the story's direction. Without even bothering with the mother or other siblings yet, we can create a dynamic by giving the father and the daughter flaws and virtues. What if she is a gifted actress, or dress designer, on the verge of a big break? Or, conversely, what if she considers herself an utter failure, and her lack of self-confidence paralyzes her? All such questions are valid and lead the story in different directions. As we develop this story, we also realize we need to learn a little more about the history of the characters, because when all is said and done, we are the products of our past. Clearly, the relationship between father and daughter is very important.

It's not necessary to solve these problems at this stage, but it is worth making a note of them as you start to create your synopsis. Gradually some ideas will mesh and you'll pursue them, while you'll discard others because they just don't fit, no matter how much you like them.

## 1.4   The Backstory: What Happened in the Past

Although the synopsis is likely to be thought out in a chronological fashion, it does not necessarily follow that the actual story should be told this way. You can split the synopsis into *backstory* and *main story*. Backstory is a scriptwriting expression, but in terms of semantics I think it's more accurate than the more commonly used "background," which does not necessarily imply *another story* (from the past) that shapes our main story. Backstory is information we will need in order for the main story to have a context, proper drama and resolution, twists and turns, irony and humor, and so forth. How to present this information in the most effective way is called *pacing of information*, which also includes using flashbacks effectively.

The following synopsis is almost a story in its own right. While most synopses are not nearly as fully developed, they will, at a minimum, sketch in a beginning, middle, and end pretty clearly. As a blueprint that sets out pieces of information to be dramatized, this synopsis will do the job fairly well. It is also perfectly okay as you write the story to alter, change, rearrange, and otherwise play with the information in the synopsis. In fact, this will probably happen during the writing process as you discover things about the characters and their relationships, conflicts, and drama in a story that a synopsis can really only suggest.

## 1.5   The Synopsis, Part 1: An Example

Here's a version of *Beauty and the Beast*. First, the backstory:

> A rich merchant and his family fell upon hard times. One day, news came that one of the merchant's ships may have survived the storm that destroyed his fleet and his fortune. His children were as excited as he at the possibility of gaining back their wealth, and all but one asked him for rich presents. The youngest, who was nicknamed Beauty for obvious reasons, asked only for a rose. Alas, by the time the merchant reached the city he found the news was false, and he was as poor as before.

Here's the main story:

> Traveling home in worsening winter weather, the merchant was forced to seek shelter in an empty but splendid

castle. Upon waking the next day, he was struck for the first time by the oddity of how the bitter winter weather had not touched the castle or its grounds. Here the sun shone, the birds sang, and flowers bloomed. It was then that he remembered his promise to bring home a rose for his youngest child.

As he gathered one, from behind him a voice roared, "Was it not enough that I gave you protection from the storm outside? Is this the way you show your gratitude, by stealing my flowers, the things I love most in the world?"

The merchant was shocked by the violence in the voice, and his shock turned to terror as he beheld the speaker, who was more beast than man. The merchant fell to his knees, begging forgiveness.

Just as the creature was about to deliver a fatal blow to the cowering merchant, however, he paused. In a calmer tone of voice, the Beast said he would not kill the merchant if, within a month, one of the merchant's daughters came of her own accord to live at the castle.

When the merchant returned home, he was greeted joyfully by his family but as he related his adventure they became horrified, turning on the youngest child and blaming her for their father's misfortune. Beauty immediately volunteered to go, and her father reluctantly accompanied her. At the castle, the Beast appeared before them and asked Beauty if she was prepared to stay. She bravely replied that she was.

And so Beauty began a lonely life amid the magnificence of the castle. At night, she dreamed about a young man who warned her not to believe her eyes, but instead trust her heart

One evening after supper she heard the Beast coming, and she was certain that something terrible was about to happen to her. He greeted her warmly, however, and Beauty was soon holding a lively conversation with the Beast, almost forgetting his fearsome mien. Every evening thereafter, the Beast came to see her; and, one night, before he bade her goodnight, he asked her to marry him.

"Oh no, I could not," she said hastily.

That night her dreams of the handsome young man changed, and he wailed about his unhappy fate that had no end in sight.

One day, the Beast asked Beauty why she was so sad. She told him she would like to see her family again.

Sighing, the Beast said he could refuse her nothing. Beauty promised that, if he let her go home, she would return in two months time to live forever in the castle. The Beast took a magic ring from his finger, gave it to Beauty, and explained that the ring would bring her safely back to him. If she failed to return as promised, though, it would cost him his life.

One night, near the end of her two-month visit, Beauty dreamed she was walking in the castle garden and heard groans coming from some bushes. Upon investigating, she discovered the Beast stretched upon his side, dying. At the same time a stately lady appeared and berated Beauty, saying, "See what happens when people do not keep their promises."

Beauty was so overcome by the dream, she hurriedly returned to the castle where she set about searching for the Beast. Inside a cave, she found him lying asleep before her. Glad to have found him, she knelt and stroked his head, but to her horror he neither awoke, moved, nor opened his eyes.

Rushing to a nearby fountain, she gathered some water and sprinkled it over his face. To her great delight he began to revive. "Oh, how you frightened me," she told him. "Do you love me then," he asked her, "ugly and fearful as I am?" and she replied that until she had seen him lying there she had not known the answer to that question. Now, she was certain that she did. "Will you marry me?" he asked her, and she replied that she would.

No sooner had she spoken than a blaze of light sprang up in the windows of the castle and fireflies spelled out, "Long live the Prince and his bride."

Turning to ask the Beast what it could all mean, Beauty found that in his place was the young man of her dreams. Beside him stood two women, one of whom was the stately woman of her dreams.

"Well, Queen," said the stately woman to her companion. "This is Beauty, whose courage finally rescued your son from his terrible enchantment."

"Now," said the woman to Beauty, "I suppose you would like me to send for your family to dance at your wedding?" And so she did. (After *La Belle et la Bête* by Madame de Villeneuve.)

In later chapters, as we discuss various ways of developing and writing a story, I'll come back to this synopsis so that you can see how theories about fiction technique are put into practice. Meanwhile, as an exercise in plotting and writing synopses, try to reduce this synopsis to its absolute bare bones. Here's a bare-bones treatment of the *Pied Piper* as an example: Town has problem with rats, man gets rid of rats, town cheats man, man steals children.

Now imagine how *Beauty and the Beast* could be told in different ways—as a horror story, for instance—or a western, science fiction, a contemporary literary novel, a romance, a mystery/thriller, and a comedy. To start you off, consider that *Beauty and the Beast* could be replotted as a werewolf or vampire tale. Does the magic have to be literal or could it be metaphorical? Is magic real, or what people believe they see, like a magician's sleight of hand?

After you've finished that exercise, write the first page for each genre of story you've plotted. Make sure you have the reader meet the protagonist almost immediately.


## 1.6 How You Tell the Story

Clearly, not all the information in the example synopsis needs to be used. Also, there's no reason, particularly for dramatic purposes, for the chronology or sequence of events to stay the same. What was the Beast's story? How did he become enchanted? Maybe Beauty isn't quite the sweet, good-natured girl she at first appears to be. What if the Beast were a woman and Beauty became Handsome, a boy, instead?

*How* you tell this story will depend on a number of choices you make: whose *point of view* you choose to tell the story, the information you select and leave out, the most dramatic way to give readers information, the personalities of the characters in your story, what you want the theme of the story to be, and so on. Most important, depending on how you answer the question *why* that keeps cropping up—why did things happen the way they did, and why did people act the way they did—you will get a coherent but very individual version of the story of *Beauty and the Beast* from each person who tackles it.

As you plot your story, you discover your characters. You take a pause from plotting to concentrate on discovering more about these characters; then you return again to plotting with a renewed sense of the actors in your drama, one element prodding the other forward in leapfrog fashion. The writing process will expand and modify all this preliminary work.


## 1.7 Exercises to Help Develop Story Sense

- After you've finished reading a novel, develop the habit of writing a 250-word review of it that (1) summarizes the story without necessarily giving the ending away, and (2) gives your opinion of whether the book is good or bad and why you think so. This is a tough exercise, but it will help to sharpen your critical faculties.

- Join a writers' group (or meet informally with other local writers), and discuss various ways to plot stories. Criticize each other's work by noting a story's strengths and weaknesses. Did the author under discussion achieve what he or she set out to achieve? And if not, why not? Discuss what you consider the story to be about. Suggest how the writer might improve his or her story. Remember, even the best writers sometimes write dreadful stories, so *don't make your criticism personal. Focus instead on the techniques used to tell a particular story.* Useful criticism is about good or bad craft and, like good editing, is a deliberate attempt to understand and clarify an author's intentions.

# 2

# "Where Do You Get Your Ideas?" Acorns into Oak Trees: The Synopsis, Part 2

> "The imagination, like the intellect, has to be used, and a creative writer ought to exercise it all the time. There is no idea, however insignificant or vague it may be, that the imagination cannot touch to new beginnings, turning it around and around in different lights, playing with it, *listening* to it."
>
> —*B. J. Chute*

Having provided an example of a synopsis in the previous chapter, let's pause here to talk about coming up with story ideas that are the basis of the synopsis. You don't have to worry about that too much if you rewrite an existing idea, such as a folk story, but what about something more original? Every author of fiction is inevitably asked the question, "Where do you get your ideas?"

The implication is that there is some sort of trick or shortcut to figuring out a good story. If only this "trick" is revealed to the questioner, he or she will be able to enter the secret, inner world of writers, dash off a best-seller, and make mounds of money.

The truth is, however, that everyone's creativity is sparked by unique circumstances that defy rational analysis. What sets one author running to the keyboard in a white heat of creativity will cause another to yawn with boredom.

The question also touches off unsettled feelings in creative people. If they're honest, they'll admit they don't really want to peer too directly into the fragile, unknown source of their creativity in case such intense scrutiny somehow causes them to lose their ability to create. There is a level of insecurity, superstition, and mysticism when one is involved in the creative process about coming up with a good idea and developing it into a story that is irrational, instinctual, and unavoidable. As a result, writers concentrate on mastering their craft and leave the visits of the muse to providence and long walks.

## 2.1   Writing What You Read

The simple answer to the question of where story ideas originate is experience. The next question is usually, "But how do I get this experience?" The answer is first to observe the world around you and start wondering and fantasizing about it; and second, read, read, and then read some more. Writing fiction is a craft, and as with any other craft, one needs to be intimately familiar with all its facets and possibilities, successes and failures. If a story satisfies you, analyze *why*. If it didn't work for you, examine that, too.

As your storytelling skills improve, you may discover that your taste in fiction changes. Novels and short stories that you earlier enjoyed no longer please you as much. They seem familiar, wooden, perhaps even clumsy. Stories and authors you didn't bother with before now catch your interest. It's a sign you're getting better at your craft because you're starting to read with discrimination and to recognize the craft of others.

Almost all writers of fiction have similar stories about how and why they started writing: They can remember the first book that grabbed them so strongly they could not put it down; and after years of starting to write stories they never finished, keeping journals, and the like, they finished reading a story by someone else and thought, "I can write something as good (or bad) as this." They then proceeded to sit down and do so.

Editors and agents repeatedly warn beginning novelists and others, "Don't write in clichés, write something original." But what does that mean? Somewhat tongue-in-cheek, but not altogether off the mark, a writer friend contends there are only two stories: a man (or woman) goes on a journey, and a stranger knocks on the door.

Originality is a twist on something familiar that makes it appear in a new light; something that hasn't been done quite that way before—a "hole," in effect. What if, as John Gardner did in his version of the *Beowulf* legend in *Grendel,* you told an old story from a fresh point of view? (Gardner used the monster's point of view, instead of the more conventional approach of using the hero's.)

Creative writing students are often told to write about what they know. What this really means, though, is write in the style of what you *read* most, and *draw upon* what you know. Is there a pattern in your reading habits? There are probably certain types of stories—romances, horror novels, spy stories, science fiction, westerns, whatever—to which you gravitate. These reading preferences are more than likely the type of story you'll try to write first.

Here are a few ways to come up with ideas for stories:

- Scour newspapers, magazines articles, and current events.

- Invent lives for strangers you see on the bus or subway or sitting across from you in a cafe.

- Consider an incident that happened to you, or someone you know, and imagine what would have happened if things had gone differently. How many times have we said to ourselves, "If only . . .?"

- Imagine what would happen if, for example, you brought home the wrong jacket from the cleaners and found something in a pocket.

- Spontaneously write an opening "hook" or sentence.

- Retell fairy tales and legends as modern stories.

As you can see, ideas are relatively easy to find once you put your mind to it. Coming up with a good one—an "original" idea—is a matter of practice, experience, and discrimination. That's where all the reading really starts to matter.

## 2.2   The Synopsis, Part 2

An idea, however, is not a story. Shaping an idea into a story is the difficult part. In the same way that an artist needs a pencil sketch to begin an oil painting, or a chef a recipe to begin cooking a meal, a writer needs a synopsis that broadly sketches out in coherent terms the essential elements of his or her story from beginning to end.

The reason some writers affect disdain for such bare-bones plotting is that it's very hard to do. They seem to forget that, beyond style, what makes the great novelists and short story writers of the past great is their *storytelling* abilities. Writers who insist they just "let the muse take them where she will" are being intellectually lazy. Certainly, one sometimes starts a story with a scene and a character with no idea where they will lead. At some point early on in the process, however, once you have discovered your fictive world and perhaps begun to explore it a little, it is essential that you plot out where you want the story to go. Such bare-bones plotting is difficult because it requires a high degree of imagination, shorn of any crutches such as a facility or gift with language, dialogue, or whatever, that you may lean upon, perhaps unconsciously, when you write fiction. Some experienced novelists may develop a story in their heads without writing it down, but one way or another they end up plotting a story before they write it. If they don't, nine times out of ten a story written in this leap-in-the-dark fashion will be long-winded, unfocused, and crippled by serious structural flaws that will need a great deal of skillful revision to fix.

(I will admit, however, that because its short length makes it harder to get into trouble technically, a short story allows a writer more leeway in leap-in-the-dark writing. Even there, however, you should at least know where you're going. This is especially true if the type of story you're writing is what James Joyce described as an "epiphany" or "moment-of-truth" story that is character-based. A great example of this is his collection of short stories, *The Dubliners*. In *The Dead*, for example, the moment of truth comes near the end, when Gabriel surprises his wife as she stands on the staircase listening to the music from upstairs; and he understands, for the first time, something fundamental about their relationship and about who she really is.)

## 2.3   Shaping Your Idea

Once ideas come to us, they must be shaped. Remember: Keep it simple. Encapsulate your idea in a sentence, or short paragraph, using one of the following phrases:

What if . . . ? or,

Suppose . . . ?

For example:

*Suppose* . . . a group of guys get together and hire a hit man to kill the president of France and then find they can't call off the assassin. (Frederick Forsyth's *The Day of the Jackal*)

*What if* . . . an Elizabethan sailor is shipwrecked off the coast of Japan and becomes a pawn in a warlord's plan to become ruler of the country? (James Clavell's *Shogun*)

One thing to notice here is that, by redefining the *idea* this way, you automatically also come up with *characters*. In the first example, the main character appears to be *the hit man*; in the second example, it seems to be *the Elizabethan sailor*. So, although I am discussing the elements of plot and character separately, they are, obviously, intimately bound together.

The only rule at the plotting stage is to get down on paper the basics of the story in a lucid manner. It's simpler and easier to take the time first to devise a rough plot synopsis. Because writing a novel is such a long process writers tend to just plow ahead until they reach "The End," only to discover real problems that they have no idea how to fix. The more novel-length projects a writer finishes, the more sense writing a synopsis makes.

A writer can become psychologically resistant to rethinking some basic elements in the book that may need fixing because of the time and effort already invested in its flawed current form. Without some kind of overview, it's easy to get hopelessly lost or sidetracked, with characters being given inappropriate prominence, or secondary plot lines becoming more important than the main story.

## 2.4 Take As Long As You Need to Plot the Story

It's okay to take months to figure out a story while a potential plot percolates around a couple of characters. Short story or novel, it's the same thing: Storytelling at this embryonic stage takes as long as it takes. Don't rush things if you don't have to. Let your subconscious do some of the work. Scenes pop up unbidden, and eventually you may be forced to accept that some elements you really wanted in the story just won't fit, and you'll have to discard them. Sometimes, the story you *thought* you were writing turns into something totally different. If you find yourself in such a situation, don't worry. This is the exploratory stage—the time for instinct to be allowed to reign unchecked, for ideas to find or repel each other, when the only rule is, There are no Rules.

It's worth remembering that no one is going to force you to stick closely to the synopsis you work out for your story. The fact is, once an idea is committed to paper, beginning writers in particular feel somehow compelled to make sure that what they've written is not wasted. It is a manifestation of the "Each-word-I-write-is-golden" and "I-may-never-write-this-well-again" syndromes, both of which are entirely false. The act of synopsizing a story from beginning to end, however broadly, will help you envision it in a useful way, even if you never look at the synopsis again.

## 2.5 Writing in Circles: Making the Connections

The best stories are circular, or spiral-like, not straight lines, so you should try to figure out these circles before sitting down to write your novel. What I mean by this is that ideally *everything* in the story should have more than one function. Once readers start to realize that a piece of plot information or a description on page 10 has a different but equally important plot function on page 30, the information is now performing *double duty*.

As you write your story, connections will occur that you did not expect. This happens because stories are organic entities that continually surprise us. Discovery is part of the fun of writing. Nevertheless, you should try to plan ahead for as many of these connections as you can. Such circular connections startle readers (in a positive way) and make them aware they can't afford to skip a single word. *That* is the real trick to creating a page turner. *Force readers to pay attention.* At the end of a novel or short story, readers should say to themselves, "Why didn't I think of that?" not, "Where did that come from?"

The synopsis establishes basic building blocks, the pieces of information readers are going to need to follow the story. Once you have figured these out, you can begin to think about the best (that is, the most entertainingly subtle) way to dramatize or "show" this information in scenes so that readers become involved with the characters and forget that the scene's purpose is to prod along the story. If you know what a scene is going to be about, in the sense that you have figured out its function in the story, you should be able to start the scene as near the action as possible (avoiding all the setup writers often feel they have to impose on readers). You can then concentrate instead on creating interesting and believable characters, while at the same time keeping the pace of the story cracking along.

## 2.6   Answering the Question Why

Another argument for doing a synopsis first is that, especially for the beginning writer of fiction, it is a worthwhile exercise in *telling* as opposed to *showing*. Tackling "show don't tell" from this perspective can be illuminating. The synopsis also helps a writer come to grips with one of the most essential elements of good storytelling: answering the question *why*.

For example: Why is this happening now and not earlier or later? Why is this character doing this or saying that? Why are they here and not there?

Each time a writer answers the question *why*, he or she learns something new about the character(s) and about the direction of the story. It is not necessarily important that *readers* always know specifically *why* something is going on; but as long as the writer knows why, the story will have an inherent cohesion that will propel it toward an inevitable conclusion. You will start to think, "Well, if she did this because of that, then it logically follows that this other thing must happen;" and the story will begin to plot itself, with nudges here and there from you.

With the average length of a novel at about 350 double-spaced manuscript pages (80–90,000 words), then the climaxes for beginning, middle, and end should roughly come at about pages 100–120, 200–220, and 340–350, respectively. Usually, the first third and last third of a book plot themselves. It is the middle of the book that more often than not gives even experienced novelists a hard time. By plotting out the story ahead of time, and pacing the development of the story and characters, much of the middle-of-the-book blues can be avoided. At the very least, the writer will have some idea of what is going to come next. Careful rereading of what you've already written will alert you to the loose threads you should pick up or snip off; and the plot synopsis can be revised accordingly.

*Here's a useful rule of thumb:*

Come up with a working title as soon as possible, because it will help to define your story and give it a central focus.

It may be that, after a while, you will discover your story needs a new title. Fine; rename it. Titling your story from the outset will give you the spine off of which you build the story's skeleton, the plot synopsis. If your story seems to be going off track, or you become confused or lost or blocked, all you need to do is step back a moment and consider the story's title. Very often, such a simple act will help things pop into perspective and solve your problems, or at least point you in the right direction.

## 2.7  Exercises to Help Develop Story Ideas

- Make a list of ten one-line ideas for stories. Then come up with a working title for each of these ideas.

- Write an opening "hook" or paragraph for each idea.

- Think of six ways you could use a golf club around the house. (This exercise is designed to stretch your imagination and force you to start thinking in original and unexpected ways.)

## 2.8  Exercises to Help Develop Synopsis Writing

- In a sentence or short paragraph beginning with "What if . . . " or "Suppose . . . ," sum up ten novels you have read. If you're unsure about how to do this, go back and look at the examples I mention in this chapter. This is not an easy exercise, but it is a worthwhile one.

- Write a synopsis (100 words or less) of each of six fairy tales. As an aid, think of how you would tell each story to a friend. Start with what really grabbed you, and then concentrate on the adventures of the main character.

- Write one story synopsis a week for at least three months—beginning, middle, and end—regardless of how good or bad it is. Keep it to a maximum of thirty double-spaced pages and a minimum of five.

- Make a list of genres, and then write a story synopsis for each one.

# 3

# Characters: The Method Writing Approach

"One never knows enough about characters. . . . [O]ne gets started and then, suddenly, one cannot remember what toothpaste they use; what are their views on interior decoration, and one is stuck utterly. . . . Major characters emerge; minor ones may be photographed."

–*Graham Greene*

As in all creative arts, technique can take you only so far. Just why one writer can create vivid characters while another succeeds only in making two-dimensional stereotypes is beyond any real analysis.

At the end of this chapter, you'll find some character notes I drew up when I first started writing fiction. Feel free to copy them if you find them useful. Filling out this character questionnaire allows the writer to keep in one place a record of whether a character has blue eyes and brown hair, or green eyes and black hair. In the case of a novel, it can help you develop in some detail a person with whom you'll be spending a lot of time and sharpen your image of a character beyond simply amassing information.

## 3.1    Writing Fiction Is about Discovery

Much of writing fiction is discovery, and that process begins with the sort of biographical details of the character(s) in your story that I've included in the questionnaire. It isn't necessary or even advisable to include in your story all the details you list. You do, however, need to know your characters so well that they seem like old friends who have stepped out of the room for a moment. You develop a feel for them, the way a good actor can say, with accuracy, "My character wouldn't say this, or do that," when confronted with out-of-character material.

This approach might be termed method writing, in the sense that we talk about method acting. You need to get inside your characters and give them lives. If you can do that, your characters' actions will portray an internal logic that often does not have to be explained.

## 3.2    Observe the World around You

To begin creating strong characters, observe the people around you and then try to distill the essence of what you see into a pithy phrase that evokes a striking image. This is easier said than done, of course. Everybody you meet is a potential character. Study the characters' general appearance, how they move, dress, talk, smell, their tones of voice or distinct styles of diction. For an exercise, spend some time people-watching in a cafe, bar, or when you're traveling, and in a small notebook make thumbnail word-sketches of the people you see. Imagine what their stories might be.

To say of a character, "He was a bear of man" (despite the fact that it's something of a cliché), is much more evocative than is a laundry list describing him as in his early thirties, six-foot-six in stockinged feet, with tattooed arms like Popeye's and a heavy brown-and-gray beard, wearing jeans and a yellow sweater but no shirt under a studded leather Hell's Angels jacket.

There is, of course, a place for such detailed description, but it should have a purpose other than to fill up space. What if our human bear also wore a ring in one ear? His tight-fitting jeans are made of shiny black leather and accentuate the bulge in his crotch. What if his hair is so dramatically close-cropped that he appears nearly bald, which accentuates his spade-shaped, salt-and-pepper beard and intense gaze?

It is not the *extent* of the details you give readers but *which* details you give that count. (There is, actually, a good rule of thumb that says never give more than three details at any one time.)

Never say a character "looked like Clint Eastwood" or was "a double for Madonna." Such descriptions are meaningless and amateurish and really turn off editors and other professional readers. Among other things, they mark you as a lazy and unimaginative writer. The only possible use for saying a character looked like Clint Eastwood would be if Eastwood were somehow featured in your story. Besides, one day there may be people who don't know what Madonna or Clint Eastwood look like. Say your novel was written forty years ago. Do you know what is meant by, "She looked like Jane Russell" or "He was as suave as Robert Donat"?

## 3.3   Characters Are Splinters of Ourselves

Characters begin as splinters of the writer's personality. Once you have a plot situation, imagine yourself in that situation. A character's fear is drawn from *your* fears. The character's hopes and delights are based on the kinds of hopes and delights *you* have experienced and can recall. Characters may be embellished and developed from observing others, but a character's emotional life starts with you.

How you nurture your characters as your story develops will greatly affect its success or failure. Regard your characters with compassion. This doesn't mean, however, that you should view them either uncritically or self-indulgently. If, for example, a character commits an immoral act, your viewing her with compassion would entail making the reader understand why she committed that act so as not to hastily condemn her as evil.

Take the point of view of a GI moving through the jungles of Vietnam. He has just learned that his wife had a miscarriage, and now he is on patrol where behind every bush the enemy may lurk. He discovers a tunnel that holds Vietcong materiel and a young woman who has just smothered her baby. His instinctive, angry reaction to his discovery is to shoot the mother. Written in a certain way, his act could be represented as sympathetic. He is a casualty of what war can do to those involved. However, if we depict this child's death as the inadvertent result of a desperate woman trying to keep her child from crying out and giving away their hiding place to armed men who terrify her, the shooting of the mother can become a trauma that haunts the GI—and perhaps your readers—for a long time.

The plot of a story is as much shaped and controlled by the characters we place in our fictional world as by the sequence of events that will be dramatized in the story. Plot and character are really indivisible elements, influencing and driving each other forward.

Sometimes you will start a story from an idea (*Suppose . . .* or *What if . . . .* ), creating characters who will make that story work. At other times, a character or characters will come first and the story develops as you explore who they are.

Once again, become flexible enough to let go of an originally inspiring idea or character in favor of a stronger idea or character that evolves beyond your initial elements. This letting go can sometimes be psychologically difficult, particularly if you find the story is not working as it should and you can't figure out exactly why.

## 3.4   First Impressions Can Be Misleading—Deliberately

In life, we judge—and often misjudge—people by first impressions. Sometimes we later readjust our impressions as we get to know them better. The same should be true of characters in fiction, if we draw them properly. For example, in London I knew a young, burly, cockney butcher with tattoos on the knuckles of his thick fingers. He had a "Gaw' blimey" attitude and his seemingly blue-collar, beer-swilling approach to life belied the fact—and quite shook me when I discovered it—that he was also a very accomplished and sensitive classical guitarist.

First impressions, prejudices, and assumptions: You can be a victim of them as a writer, thereby perpetuating two-dimensional stereotypes, or you can make them work for you. (P. D. James's detective character, Adam Dalgleish, for example, is a senior British homicide detective who is also a recognized, serious poet, not what you would expect from a police officer if you only write in clichés. Len Deighton's unnamed spy—they called him Harry Palmer in the movies— in the *Ipcress File*, *Funeral in Berlin*, and others, was a gourmet cook, even though he was British working class, a former army noncom, and therefore was expected to be uncouth and live on fish and chips and pints of beer.)

## 3.5  Make the Character Fit the Story

To make your story credible, a character has to be able to perform the actions sketched out in your plot synopsis. Simply put, you wouldn't create a character like Mark Twain's Huck Finn, use him as the lead character (John Rambo) in David Morrel's *First Blood*, and expect the story to be either convincing or successful. On the face of it, such a point seems obvious, even ludicrous, and yet writers do similar things all the time.

Here's an example of what I mean: A pudgy young woman lives alone with three cats. She knows she is constantly short-changed by the brash young man at the local deli who always seems to be making fun of her to the other customers while she's waiting to be served, but she continues to shop there without ever complaining. Old ladies push her out of the way as they jump the queue to get on the bus ahead of her. Her boss forever makes her make coffee for him, do his errands, and then makes her stay late to finish the work she couldn't get done during the day. She goes home and throws things around, screams and cries, but in public she is always meek and mild. She is one of life's victims, and perhaps a little unstable.

One evening on her way home from work, she is pulled into an alleyway and attacked by three tough young men. Without any warning our mousy secretary suddenly explodes with aggression and becomes a killer kung fu expert, in short order putting all three young men in the hospital.

However well you write that action scene, you have established only that our heroine is mousy and repressed. She may be a bomb ready to explode from the frustrations and indignities life has heaped upon her. Nevertheless, the reader has been given no earlier clue or indication that she is capable of acting violently towards others, let alone being skilled in martial arts. Such behavior is so out of character readers will be jolted from the fictional dream you are creating. You will lose your audience and fail as a storyteller. You can surprise readers, but they must also say to themselves, "Oh, that's clever. Now, why didn't I think of that?"

## 3.6 Writing Is Making and Solving Puzzles

Writing stories is to a large degree making puzzles and solving them, even when the story is a literary novel. One way you might solve the writing problem I've just described is to create a couple of scenes early on in which our secretary takes a course in karate. That kind of solution, however, strikes me as being an obvious (and rather boring) approach to the problem and, even then, is not a terribly believable solution. One needs to have practiced martial arts for many years before it is useful in such a street situation.

What if, however, you write an early scene or two in which *something* so terrifies the secretary that it represents a catharsis that prompts her to action? In desperation she buys a handgun and ammunition. Now we are beginning to develop a story from a character. Handled properly, the reader's initial sympathy for the secretary turns to unease. Perhaps this unstable person will now unleash her frustration with violence towards the wrong people. Before the reader's eyes, like Dr. Jekyll becoming Mr. Hyde, the secretary gradually turns into a walking time bomb. It is only a matter of time before she uses that loaded weapon in her purse.

You can imagine the rest of the story. In fact, as an exercise, you might wish to write a short story using variations on the above ideas. Will she kill the young men when she is assaulted? Or will the ingrained fears of a lifetime win out and make her helpless at the critical moment? If the incident took place in a subway car instead of an alleyway, and she uses the gun, is an innocent bystander hurt? How does she react to accidentally shooting and maiming a fourteen-year-old girl who is on her way to night school?

Take a look at Stephen King's first novel, Carrie, to see how he handled this type of story.

## 3.7   Character Is Revealed through Conflict

Several important lessons can be drawn from the previous scenario:

> First, no piece of fiction will work if the central character is passive. The protagonist of a story *must* have a goal and *must* be the agent of his or her struggle to attain that goal. In other words, the protagonist must *do* things, not just have things happen to him or her.
>
> Second, character is revealed through conflict. People reveal their true selves under pressure.

Strong stories show how characters confront and resolve moral and ethical dilemmas. Written well, an action scene may hold us for a half dozen pages. For example, in the classic melodrama, will our hero get to the railway tracks in time to untie the heroine from the rails before the train flattens her? Confront the same hero with having to choose between saving his sister, or his wife and child, and, properly developed, you can hold readers for as many as fifty pages.

Confronting a protagonist (or antagonist) with moral and ethical dilemmas is the most effective way to hold your readers' interest because they can more readily identify with the trauma of the situation. The reader becomes a participant in the story rather than a passive observer and, as a result, will care more about how the story is resolved.

## 3.8   Show, Don't Tell–1

It is not enough to invent a history, physical characteristics, and feelings for a character and then just tell this information to the reader. Character is best portrayed by *actions* or *deeds*, and these are determined by the *type* of character you have created. The difference between the readers' determining the kind of person a character is from his actions, and having the character or the author explain or narrate directly to the reader what the character is doing and why is what I mean by the rule, "Show, don't tell." Always strive for the *external demonstration* of a character's thoughts and feelings, rather than the internalized voice explaining these thoughts and feelings.

The plotting possibilities that stem from a character's actions multiply when a writer uses questions as a prompt in building a story outline, in particular the question *why.*

Remember this rule of thumb:

Plot is what characters do next.

All good stories are, in a sense, *biographies* that encompass key events, milestones, or watersheds in a person's life. Characters—particularly protagonists but also sometimes antagonists—should change from the beginning of the story to the end. Your story is, on one level, the narrative of the journey of that change. This is true even in such fiction genres as mysteries, thrillers, and romances. (It's especially true of romances because they chart one of the most important watershed moments in a person's life, the time he or she finds true love.)

## 3.9   The Protagonist Should Change

Heroes and heroines shouldn't just survive their adventure, ending it by finding a solution to the puzzle with which they've been confronted. The solution to that puzzle should come from the main character's growing awareness of his condition. That is, the character should arrive at a new appreciation of his circumstances and/or the circumstances of those around him. Good examples of this are Scrooge in Charles Dickens's *A Christmas Carol* or Charlie, the central character in Daniel Keyes's award-winning novella *Flowers for Algernon*.

It bears repeating that the success of your story is largely dependent on the depth of attention you pay to characterization. In general, the more you focus the reader's attention and tell (i.e., narrate) a story from a single point of view, the more successful the story. The corollary is also true: The less you focus on a single character whose story you are—or should be— telling, and the more points of view you use, the less successful your story because it will be less emotionally involving and more scattershot in its narrative sweep.

## 3.10   Use the Right Tools for the Job

Inexperienced writers often make the mistake of trying to write short books using epic techniques, which are simply the wrong tools for the job. The epic novel of 1,000 printed pages, such as *Shogun* or *War and Peace*, has the room to follow three or four major characters without confusing readers by skipping from character to character. Confusion is exactly what results when you use epic techniques for a 350–400-page manuscript. There are obvious exceptions to this generalization, but, by and large, the rule of thumb is:

Keep it small, keep it simple, keep the focus tight.

In general, it is very hard for a first novelist to get published any work shorter than 250 double-spaced manuscript pages (about 70,000 words) or more than 450 double-spaced manuscript pages (about 100,000 words). [While these length limits are arbitrary, they have as much to do with the economics of book publishing as with anything else.]

## 3.11    How to Judge a Story's Success

A story's success is judged more by the strength of its villain (i.e., antagonist) than by that of its hero. One defines the other. Your hero achieves less by overcoming an opponent or obstacle that is weak or two-dimensional. He or she has less to lose, and, consequently, the story is not compelling. We all have a touch of both hero and villain within us, and the better stories reflect this paradox. Oversimplified, this means that heroes should have clay feet while villains should be, in some measure, likeable.

William Faulkner said, "A writer must teach himself that the basest of all things is to be afraid." Another way of putting it is, "Don't let your mother look over your shoulder when you are writing." In other words, don't let the judgment of others inhibit your writing. If you're not careful, you'll start to think a relative or friend may believe something you have written is an offensive comment about him or her, and it will hamper your storytelling ability. As a rule, writers draw upon their life experiences. They don't recreate these experiences in fiction exactly as they happened. Instead, they use them as a springboard to something they have imagined.

Albert Camus once said, "A guilty conscience needs to confess. A work of art is a confession." Elia Kazan put it this way, "The writer, when he is also an artist, is someone who admits what others don't dare reveal."

Come to grips with your own faults, fears, and hopes in

order to write with insight about those of other people. Without admitting to and exploring your own dark nature, you will never successfully understand it in others. I am not suggesting you must become a Nazi or a cannibalistic serial killer in order to successfully create them as fictional characters. I *am* suggesting that you try to find that part of yourself that, *under certain circumstances you could imagine* going berserk and committing singularly antisocial acts.

## 3.12   Do the Right Thing

Writing realistic fiction can be, psychologically, a very sobering experience. Serious storytellers are compelled to discover within themselves dark feelings and thoughts that, through the deeds of their characters, force both writer and reader to admit that life is a continual struggle to act decently and do the right thing.

In this regard, it is interesting to read some Freud, some Jung (who had a long friendship and correspondence with the novelist Herman Hesse, author of *Steppenwolf* and *Siddhartha*, among others), Wilhelm Reich (particularly *Character Analysis* and *The Mass Psychology of Fascism*), and some biographies. Although this approach to creating characters can be taken too far, it helps you understand human nature, people's dreams and fears, and why they do some of the things they do. Successful storytellers are also students of human nature.

Here now are some examples of how successful writers introduce us to some of their characters. The first example is also the opening paragraph of Ronald Hardy's novel, *The Wings of the Wind*:

This was the second day of their escape and when the light began to fade Lewis Mackenna drove the truck up the rise of the ground to where the camphor trees grew. He positioned the truck so that it would not be seen from the road or from the air and when the engine was switched off he sat for a time immersed in the silence of the wild land. He heard Ellen Mackenna stir beside him and, turning, he watched her awaken. He stroked her cheek. He could see the imprint of exhaustion on her face. They had driven through the previous night and then through the yellow heat of the day. He again felt the onset of fear. What have I done to them? he asked himself; these three lives. He pulled her toward him and their sweating faces slid together. There was movement in the rear and he looked across the crown of her sleeping head. But the two boys had not awakened.

Apart from the real grace of the prose style, what makes this a wonderful opening paragraph is that we learn so much about Lewis Mackenna and his situation without even realizing it. It immediately plunges us into the fictional world, grabbing us from the moment the story begins. He's in a "wild land"— China, we later learn—and he is on the run (Whom does he fear?) in a truck with his wife and two children. He is frightened and clearly in serious trouble, but he is struggling with his fears, which is the sign of a man of courage. He loves his wife and kids; he is a man capable of tenderness and, implicitly, compassion, and he blames himself for whatever terrible misfortune he senses is about to befall them. What could such a man have done to get himself into this awful predicament? Ronald Hardy, an American master craftsman of fiction, is unfortunately ignored. A *New York Times* review once rightly described his work as "simply staggering . . . awesome authority." I recommend you go out of your way to find his work and read it.

In *The Book of Daniel*, E. L. Doctorow presents one of his characters this way:

Asher's huge hand was like a band of steel. He was a gentle, soft spoken man, but when he was excited he lost control of his great strength and didn't know he was using it. Daniel tried to pull away, to loosen the ring of pain around his wrist, but Asher's response was to tighten his grip and pull even harder. "Come, children, come," the lawyer said. Laboriously they scrambled up the steps from the subway—a steep flight encased in black dirt and littered with gum wrappers and flattened cigarette butts.

*Daniel*, which Doctorow wrote before he wrote his best-selling novel *Ragtime*, is a fictional recreation of the Julius and Ethel Rosenberg treason case of the early 1950s. It is told from the point of view of Daniel, one of the two Rosenberg children, who have been adopted by the Rosenbergs' friend and lawyer, Asher, after their parent's execution. The contrast between a caring, intelligent man and one who, when excited, hurts the very people he is trying so hard to care for, is an excellent thumbnail characterization which tells us as much about Daniel's childhood experiences as about Asher and life in general.

Here is how Joyce Carol Oates begins her novel *Solstice*:

It was on a mild, fragrant evening in late September, several weeks after she had moved to Glenkill, Pennsylvania, to begin teaching at the Glenkill Academy for Boys, that Monica Jensen was introduced to Sheila Trask at a crowded reception in the headmaster's residence. And the meeting was so awkward, her own response so lacking in brilliance or distinction, Monica could never have predicted that Sheila Trask would remember her, or even that they would see each other again.

Note how this opening paragraph immediately plunges us into Monica's world and gives us a strong sense of her nagging insecurity. The introduction is portentous and makes us want to see not only what will become of Monica, but discover as well who Sheila Trask is and how she will change Monica's life. Monica, in a sense, is everywoman. Sheila, by contrast, is set up to be someone Monica aspires to emulate. (". . . her own response so lacking in brilliance or distinction, Monica could never have predicted that Sheila Trask would remember her . . .") As Oates subtly delves deeper, we realize that, because Sheila Trask *does* remember Monica, Monica must be more interesting than she believes herself to be. A page or so later we encounter this description:

> By the time of the Greenes' party, months later, Monica had quite forgotten about Sheila Trask . . . . So when, at the Greenes' spirited party, she had happened to see a tall, dark-haired, rather slovenly dressed woman enter the room, Monica had thought only that she was odd—arresting—a "character" in some not fully tangible way. She was a woman five or six years older than Monica, in her midthirties perhaps, and attractive enough, even—almost—beautiful, with derisive black eyes and heavy unplucked black brows and a wide, unsmiling, quizzical mouth. Her figure was almost painfully angular; her shoulders were sloping, her posture slouched. Unlike the Greenes' other guests she had not taken the occasion seriously enough to dress for it—she wore a shapeless black skirt that fell unevenly to midcalf, and a cheap much-laundered cotton shirt, and what appeared to be a man's tweed jacket, unbuttoned, and drooping from her thin shoulders. An odd bird of prey, Monica thought.

Apart from the general atmosphere created here, and despite the fact that the author describes Sheila Trask with more than three details (as I previously suggested), each detail contributes to the story and piques the reader's interest. There are, for example, the "derisive black eyes," the "painfully angular" figure, the fact that Monica considers Sheila a "bird of prey." Who would not want to know more about these two women and how their lives will intertwine?

A quite different method of characterization can be found in Pat Conroy's *The Prince of Tides*.

> When I was ten I killed a bald eagle for pleasure, for the singularity of the act, despite the divine, exhilarating beauty of its solitary flight over schools of whiting. It was the only thing I had ever killed that I had never seen before. After my father beat me for breaking the law and for killing the last eagle in Colleton County, he made me build a fire, dress the bird, and eat its flesh as tears rolled down my face. Then he turned me in to Sheriff Benson, who locked me in a cell for over an hour. My father took the feathers and made a crude Indian headdress for me to wear to school. He believed in expiation of sin.

In Conroy's brief but complete characterization, we learn what seems to be the narrator's worst childhood experience (which will later prove not to be the case) and also a great deal about his father *and* their relationship.

Finally, this excerpt from *The Vampire Lestat* by Anne Rice which begins downtown in a nameless city on a Saturday night in 1984:

> I am the Vampire Lestat. I'm immortal. More of less. The light of the sun, the sustained heat of an intense fire—these things might destroy me. But then again, they might not.
>
> I'm six feet tall, which was fairly impressive in the 1780s when I was a young mortal man. It's not bad now. I have thick blond hair, not quite shoulder length, and rather curly, which appears white under fluorescent light. My

eyes are gray, but they absorb the colors blue or violet easily from surfaces around them. And I have a fairly short narrow nose, and a mouth that is well shaped but just a little too big for my face. It can look very mean, or extremely generous, my mouth. It always looks sensual. . . .

## 3.13   Naming Characters

We should spend a moment discussing the names you give your characters. Characters' names *do* make a difference. *Your* associations with those names are likely to be different from those of your readers. Whereas in a nineteenth-century historical novel, you could name your characters Demis, Erastus, Sophronia, and the like, except to achieve a specific effect, you wouldn't want to give such names to modern characters. If you did, would Erastus be a judge or a bishop from an old New England family? While the name "Percy" can work well in a historical novel, it might suggest a somewhat weak personality in a modern novel.

Alliteration in names generally seems too forced and can be distracting to readers. Besides, how many people do you know whose names are Anthony Andrews or Debbie Daniels? Also, try not to give characters last names that sound like first names, such as Bob James. Should an anorexic character be named Bertha? Why not? Would you call a cowboy from the Southwest "Ernest"? Ernie, maybe. Then again, perhaps he's very formal and precise and Ernest is exactly what he should be named. Chuck, not Chas, Charles, or Charlie? Don't give *different* characters names that start with the same initials, or sound the same. Why confuse readers unnecessarily with a hero called Arnold Samuels and a villain's henchman called Arty Sampson?

Consider names carefully. They not only shape the reader's

image of your character, they add to or conflict with the mental picture you are creating. Unconsciously, when you name a character, you are placing a clue to that character's nature into the name. Sometimes you may want to name your characters "against type," as with a cowboy named Ernest. You could name a member of the British upper classes Priscilla, perhaps, but you'd have to be pretty off the mark to marry a European aristocrat to someone named Betty Sue. (Unless, of course, Betty Sue is a pig-tailed American girl who captivates the aristocrat.) The purpose in finding the right names for your characters is to avoid distracting the reader from the story. Bland or inappropriate character names simply confuse the reader.

In a story, names are never neutral. They always signify something. In *Martin Chuzzlewit*, for example, Charles Dickens describes General Fladdock as "a starched and punctilious American militia officer." He also calls Mr. Lewsome "a degraded assistant to a London general practioner." Lewsome, of course, puts the reader in mind of the word "lewd." Fladdock conjures up flatulence and coarse excess. Dickens's characters' names, deliberately satirical and extreme, tell his readers much about the characters in stories that sometimes feature ten or more important characters. Consider why Edgar Allan Poe chose the name William Wilson for the hero of his story "Doppelgänger." Could he, perhaps, have been giving us a clue to solve the riddle of his story by naming his hero with first and last names that almost seemed to echo each other as do the two characters? The word "doppelgänger" means the ghostly double of a living person.

## 3.14   Exercises to Help Create Characters

• Write biographies for several characters who might be protagonists and antagonists in some of your stories.

Develop characters for some of the synopses you wrote in the exercises in Chapter 1.

- Create characters using the questionnaire that follows and try to invent stories that derive from their lives.

- Scene: A woman with a baby in a backpack gets onto a subway train, sits down and starts to read. A youth comes up to her and asks her the time. She ignores him and pointedly continues to read. Write this scene in the first person from the woman's point of view, the youth's point of view, the point of view of a third person observing them.

- Find names for the following characters:

  1. A college-educated but amoral thief who can't hold down a job

  2. A mother who is jealous of her daughter's success after having relentlessly pushed the daughter to the heights of success while showing little regard for what the daughter really wanted

  3. A young man who, against all odds, has just been asked to join a minor league baseball team

  4. An attractive, ambitious woman executive who is making life for her staff very difficult

  5. The ambitious executive's personal assistant

  6. A female firefighter

A character questionnaire follows. My purpose is not to make you crazy finding answers to all the questions. Answer as many or as few as you like. The objective is to get your creative juices flowing and help you focus or define more clearly your ideas about a character. Furthermore, the questionnaire can help you make sure you don't have two characters in a story who are accidentally similar in either name, character, or description.

## 3.15   A Sample Character Questionnaire

### Character Notes

Name:
Job:
*Physical description*
Age:
Height:
Weight:
Hair (style and color):
Eyes:
Voice:
*Scars and handicaps*
Physical:
Emotional:
Sort of home lived in (feel of it):
*Key dates/events in character's life*
Background:
Born (date):
Birthplace:
Astrological sign:
Parents:
Brothers and sisters:
Marital status:
Spouse name:
Children (names and ages):
Most important influences:
*Education*
School:

College:

University:

Other:

*Work experience*

First job:

Others:

Present job:

*Psychological Profile/Other notes*

Philosophy of life:

Ambitions:

Fantasies/daydreams:

Favorite color:

Character's aura: animal or object?:

Closest friend(s):

Acquaintances:

Enemies:

Is afraid of:

Sees self as:

Is seen as:

Best character traits:

Worst character traits:

Most important thing to know about character:

Character's darkest secret:

Descriptive word or phrase on seeing character for first time:

How character reacts to peers' views of character:

How far character will go to get what he or she wants:

Problems at the story's beginning:

Present problem:

How it will get worse:

## Bio

(Write a one-page character biography based on the information you used to complete the questionnaire.)

# 4

# Actors in Action: Characters' Deeds and Needs

"Writers seldom choose as friends those self-contained characters who are never in trouble, never unhappy or ill, never make mistakes and always count their change when it's handed to them."

—*Catherine Drinker Bowen*

If *"plot" is what characters do next*, then the most effective fiction creates strong characters whose actions naturally move the story along. Ideally, everything in your fiction should give the reader information that advances the story while at the same time foreshadows something else that will make sense to a reader later on. This is not an easy task, of course, and takes considerable thought. Sometimes it is simplest just to follow your story outline, and then in revision compress and reshape the information.

## 4.1 Capturing the Inner Movie

The success of a story can be measured by how accurately you can capture on paper in a cinematic way (that is, in dramatically observed scenes) the "movie" (i.e., story) that is taking shape in your imagination. The less a writer tells readers what a character is thinking, and the less he describes one character's relationship to another, the stronger will be the story. Fiction writers should concentrate on finding the most dramatic way of showing us a character's inner life so that readers can discover it for themselves. To do this, you must make sure that the information you want to share with your readers is relevant and therefore worth the trouble of dramatizing.

Use a journalistic approach rather than an "inner monologue" style. Readers usually don't respond well to an author acting as an interpreter of the action because it intrudes and disturbs the fictive dream taking shape. This "navel gazing" approach transforms your readers from active participants to passive observers. An objective observational approach makes for more effective storytelling because it allows readers to participate in the story.

For example:

> "Damn her for what she's done to me. How am I going to deal with this?" thought George angrily,

is passable storytelling, but *tells* us a lot more than it *shows* us. Now, this:

> "Damn you," George shouted. "Now what the hell am I going to do?" Without warning he punched a hole through the kitchen's plasterboard wall. Emily backed against the door, her hands shaking as they covered her mouth.

While this scene, taken out of context, is somewhat melodramatic, it is on the whole more effective than the previous one because we get a sense of what both George *and* Emily are thinking and feeling through their *actions*, rather than through the author telling us directly he was angry, she was scared. It avoids the clumsy he-thought-she-thought technique that distances and confuses readers because there is no touchstone or frame of reference (i.e., whom should the reader root for?) in the scene. In the same way that character and plot are intertwined, dramatizing your story is intimately bound up with *viewpoint*.

Ideally, you should use a mixture of both techniques, giving readers only the most important thoughts of the protagonist, and maybe antagonist, while limiting yourself to showing only the end results of the thoughts of other characters.

## 4.2 Leave Out the Parts Readers Skip

Like sorting wheat from chaff, you must decide which details are important to your story and which merely set the scene, and then determine how best to dramatize the important points. The choices you make allow you to control exactly what you want your readers to discover and when they discover it. Important details shouldn't become buried under a mass of trivial detail that quickly becomes tiresome to read. If you write this way, a reader is forced to filter out much of this trivia in search of the story, and as a result will also begin to miss the important information needed to make sense of your story. When asked to explain the success of his detective novels, Elmore Leonard said, "I leave out the parts people skip."

*Try this exercise:*

In half a page or so, describe a house as seen by a very angry man. Do not mention the man, his anger, or why he is angry. Now describe the same house as seen by a young girl glad to be home. Don't mention her or her feelings, either.

## 4.3   Start with a Character, Not a Place

The "trick" to the foregoing exercise is knowing something about the character doing the viewing, because description is a function of viewpoint. *It is not the author doing the describing, but the character.* Description is not simply something that sits on the page setting the scene like a lump in gravy. One of the major mistakes inexperienced writers make is to start a story with a description and not action. Establishing a sense of place and time may help a writer get going in a first draft, but that doesn't mean that's where the story should start in the final version. *What* we are shown is very much a function of character, so briefly introduce readers to the character who is doing the viewing, *before* showing in detail what that character sees.

## 4.4   Sources of Dramatic Conflict

People do things for a reason, however deep-seated and unconscious the motivation. *Everything has a purpose to a character.* It is human nature to act from need or desire. Once you know what a character wants and the intensity of that desire, you can figure out whether he is the sort of person who will go to any length to get it, or if he will draw a line at some point if success means overstepping personal moral or ethical boundaries, or whether fear of failure freezes him into inactivity, and the like.

Conflict, and therefore story, spring from the many internal forces that drive us to say and do things. These forces include desires and wants, dreams and fantasies, dark secrets and fears we want to suppress, perhaps even from our own consciousness. The playwright Harold Pinter says dramatic conflict is created by the threats that arise when people in a confined space battle for dominance of each other. The characters have a clearly defined purpose: the search for "tools" that will help them achieve their own dominance while at the same time undermine the growing dominance of other characters. Pinter's insights about the dynamics of a scene seem to me to be a fundamental element of good storytelling, whether in plays and screenplays or short stories and novels.

## 4.5  Make Your Character Act

If a novelist knows *why* a character acts as she does, even if, as is likely, the character herself is ignorant of what motivates her, then the character will always make sense. This is true even when the story is told from a viewpoint that does not permit readers to hear directly that character's thoughts or know her feelings. If readers really need to be told these thoughts and feelings, the writer should dramatize them. Make your character *act*, don't explain her to the reader.

For example, in Thomas Harris's best-selling novel *Red Dragon* (which preceded *The Silence of the Lambs* and was made into the movie *Manhunter*), the main motivation of the protagonist, FBI serial killer expert Will Graham, is his struggle with a secret terror that, deep down, he is a serial killer who has never acted upon his impulses. That's why he believes he is so uncannily good at getting inside the minds of the mass murderers he tracks. Acts that to most cops seem random make sense to Graham. When Graham comes out of retirement and visits the psychopathic serial killer Hannibal Lecter (who first appeared in *Red Dragon*) to "get the mindset back," Harris creates a chilling confrontational scene that portrays Graham's fear instead of simply describing it. Lecter's brilliant intellect homes in on this weakness of Graham's, and he taunts Graham with it. Lecter verbalizes Graham's secret torment (that the only reason he was able to capture Lecter was because Graham is just like him). Thus something vital about Graham is revealed to the reader with drama, not description.

At one point in *Red Dragon*, in discussing the serial killer he is chasing, a policeman, horrified, says to Will Graham, "You feel sorry for this monster?" to which Graham replies in effect, "I mourn for the child who was so brutally treated, not the man he became who is now beyond redemption." This is complex characterization that gains from an avoidance of gory or "splatter" writing. (In all fairness, however, it's worth pointing out there is a new school of modern fiction called the "splatterpunk" school, fashioned after similarly violent and gory movies, though it is already falling out of fashion.)

## 4.6 Dialogue

Dialogue, defined as what people say and how they say it, is a way to show character. It develops and defines character and can contradict a character's actions. Quite often what we *say* and what we *do* may not match. Sometimes, also, what's not said is more important than what is said. If dialogue is well written, it is rarely necessary to embellish it with an adjective or adverb.

In, *"You bastard!" he said angrily*, the adverb "angrily" is redundant. There is also no need to italicize words, use exclamation marks, or employ any other tool of emphasis unless to indicate the speaker is shouting. People generally use language like that only if they are angry, so the qualification is redundant. *"You bastard," he said*, is enough.

*"You bastard," he said, laughing*, however, does *not* qualify but describe, because it is, on the face of it, contradictory to the implications of the dialogue.

There are some writers who have a gift for capturing speech in written form. It's as though they can replay the essence of a conversation without the hesitations and nonessential words that most of us use, yet convey the verisimilitude of eavesdropping. Ed McBain (Evan Hunter), Elmore Leonard, Charles

Dickens, and Toni Morrison are fiction writers with this gift who are worth studying.

As an exercise, tape yourself and a friend discussing something (perhaps over the phone), then transcribe it. Now try to boil the conversation down to its essence without losing the personality of the speakers. This is much harder than it seems, but may well give you a good insight into what does and does not work on the page.

When writing dialogue, keep in mind that people rarely explain themselves. They often reveal as much about themselves by what they *don't say*, as they do by what they do talk about. A sure way to make a character dull and uninteresting (and bore readers to death in the process) is to have the character spout messages, oratory, and exposition. Instead of *showing* your story, you're merely *telling* your story through dialogue. The fact is, most people are inarticulate or vague, especially when explaining what motivates them to act. Does this sound familiar?

"Why did you break that vase, Jimmy?"

"I dunno."

"What do you mean, you don't know. You must know. You're old enough to start taking some responsibility for a change. I can't leave you alone for a second, can I? That vase belonged to my grandmother. I've told you before about playing ball indoors, haven't I?"

Jimmy shrugged, staring at his unlaced sneakers. He seemed intent on scuffing one against the other.

"Goddamnit, pay attention when I'm talking to you. Well?"

Although this is pretty expositional, the writer isn't being overly obvious. Because the adult's angry speech is close enough to what is considered real speech in such a situation, the information conveyed in the scene is not what first catches our eye. Our main focus is on how the scene will develop in terms of the conflict between the adult and the child. This snippet of characterization through dialogue takes on different hues when we place it in a specific context.

Consider what might happen if the speakers are mother and son in their own home; or if they are staying with a relative because they have nowhere else to go; or if the woman is looking for a reason to leave her son with an unsuspecting friend or relative, and the boy knows this. Or perhaps the boy is reacting to a stepmother he resents.

Note how Eudora Welty used dialogue effectively in her short story "Why I Live at the P.O.":

> Soon as [my sister Stella Rondo] got married and moved away from home the first thing she did was separate! From Mr. Whitaker! This photographer with the popeyes she said she trusted. Came home from one of those towns in Illinois and to our complete surprise brought this child of two.
>
> Mama said she like to made her drop dead for a second. "Here you had this marvelous blonde child and never so much as wrote your mother a word about it," says Mama. "I'm thoroughly ashamed of you." But of course she wasn't.
>
> Stella Rondo just calmly takes off this *hat*, I wish you could see it. She says, "Why, Mama, Shirley-T.'s adopted, I can prove it."
>
> "How?" says Mama, but all I says was, "H'm!"

As an exercise, write a piece of dialogue between two characters in which each character has a secret he or she must keep from the other. Avoid the temptation to explain any but the most important observable detail (what a character does when he or she has nothing to say in reply). After you've written that, read O. Henry's short story "The Gift" to see what he did with this idea.

It concerns a poor husband and wife buying Christmas

presents for each other. He sells his watch to buy her a beautiful comb for her long hair, which she has cut off and sold in order to buy him a chain for his watch.

## 4.7  When to Use Dialogue

Knowing when to use dialogue is governed by the rule "Show, don't tell." If, in the course of a scene, a character meets a female friend and learns from her that his wife has been spotted in another man's car, what we want to dramatize is not the "fat," or exchange of pleasantries at the beginning, but the "meat," or emotional heart of the scene.

> Later that afternoon Chas and Susie met again and paused for a few moments outside the supermarket, shooting the breeze. Susie was friendly enough, but kept fidgeting and looking over Chas's shoulder, as though distracted and waiting to leave. Finally, Chas said, "Are you okay?"

This is obviously where the dialogue would begin.

In narrative you might write, *Lori was concerned about how Joe was getting on.* As dialogue, you might write, *"Are you okay, Joe?"*

Whatever is most immediate and straightforward tends to be the best rule of thumb in choosing when to dramatize dialogue and narrative. There is a difference between saying:

> They had the most awful row that afternoon, and Richard stormed out of the house,

which should probably be dramatized in some fashion; and,

> For the next six months, Richard and Amy did nothing but argue, or so it seemed to Lawrence. He was not sur-

prised to return home one day just as Richard barged past him out of the house, threatening divorce over his shoulder.

In the first example, the important piece of information is the row that caused Richard to leave. In the second, it is the pattern of arguments over time, not a single pivotal argument that, seen through the eyes of an observer, is probably a bridging passage from one scene in the story to another, and so could be left in its present form.

## 4.8   Some of the Pitfalls of Writing Dialogue

Avoid too much direct address dialogue: "Well, Ethel," "Yes, Sidney," type of stuff. Avoid also expository and stilted dialogue: "Is that a huge gun I see in your hand, William?" "Yes, I'm pleased you noticed. I intend to shoot you with it." Avoid unnecessary dialogue:

"Hello, Chris."
"Hello, Stacy. How are you?"
"I'm fine, how are you?"
"Good. How's your mother?"
"She's fine. And yours?"
"Okay. How's your dad?"
"Okay. And the dog?"
"Not so good. How's the cat?"

What have we learned from this dialogue? The answer is absolutely nothing, so why waste readers' time with it? Just so you can claim your novel is "realistic"? In all likelihood, readers would skip passages like this as they search for the next part of the story that propels the plot forward. Or, they might skip the rest of the story.

Every time a person speaks, she reveals an aspect of her personality. Avoid "ums" and "ers," and funny quirks and accents except to briefly set the scene. Remember, keep it simple.

The best way to give readers a sense of accent or dialect is to plant simple clues or signposts that alert them to what is going on and helps them listen to the characters with their inner ear without making reading an arduous experience. The mistake that novice writers often make is to try to catch literally on paper the sound of the accent or dialect, rather than merely to suggest it by using recognizable language. For example:

"Whewl, thar I wuz, stan'in' in me whistle 'n flute waitin' f'ra bloody pub daws t'op'n to passatime afore the weddin' when . . ."

It is better written as:

"Well, there I was, standing in me whistle and flute [cockney rhyming slang for suit] for the bloody pub doors to open to pass the time before the wedding when . . ."

In the following excerpt, taken from *Jazz* by Toni Morrison, note how masterfully the author uses subtle rhythms of phrase and sentence in her dialogue, and a precise choice of language, to achieve a strong sense of dialect. We are in Harlem in the late 1920s.

The sister was screaming in front of her house, drawing neighbors and passersby to her as she scanned the sidewalk—up and down—shouting "Philly! Philly's gone! She took Philly!" She kept her hands on the baby buggy's push bar, unwilling to run whichever way her gaze landed, as though, if she left the carriage, empty except for the record she dropped in it—the one she had dashed back into the house for and that was now on the pillow where her baby brother used to be—maybe it too would disappear.

"She who?" somebody asked. "Who took him?"

"A woman! I was gone one minute. Not even one! I asked her . . . I said . . . and she said okay . . . !"

"You left a whole live baby with a stranger to go get a record?" The disgust in the man's voice brought tears to the girl's eyes. "I hope your mama tears you up and down."

Opinions, decisions popped through the crowd like struck matches.

"Ain't got the sense of a gnat."

"Who misraised you?"

"Call the cops."

"What for?"

"They can at least look."

"Will you just look at what she left that baby for."

"What is it?"

"The Trombone Blues."

"Have mercy."

"She'll know more about the blues than any trombone when her mama gets home."

By comparison, here is how David Bradley portrays black idiom in his prize-winning novel, *The Chaneysville Incident*. An old southern black man describes what happened the night he fell into the hands of the Ku Klux Klan:

"They put us up in front of a bunch of 'em an' they made us march. Josh coulda run, maybe, but he looked deader'n a two-day-old catfish, an' I wasn't gonna get too far wearin' eighty pounds a chain. So we jest walked along, me keepin' my eyes peeled for a sign a Mose. I figgered he had to be doin' somethin', an' I knowed it wasn't goin' for no sheriff. But he didn't show hisself, an' nothin' happened. So all I could do was march."

Although Bradley pushes the language and the rhythm a bit, at no point is what we are reading unclear or unintelligible, and the character's voice and personality come through distinctly. Note too, here and in the following examples, how the names of the characters also help to set up images of them.

Michael Weston creates small-town, suspicious tin miners in nineteenth-century Cornwall, England, in *The Cage*, winner of the 1986 Georgette Heyer Historical Novel Prize. Although Weston makes even more demands on the reader's participation than does Bradley, again it's successful because it doesn't take much to understand what the characters are saying once the reader is tuned in to the way they speak. Despite the dialect and language, we still have a clear idea of what is being said, who is saying it, and of time and place. Clarity is uppermost.

> "There's a better smith in Windfall than Tom Magor, so they tell me," Hilda Trérice was saying quietly.
> "Who said that? I'll beat 'is brains out," blustered Magor.
> "More'n one 'ave said it, ever since that Welland—"
> "Oh, Welland! Welland!" he broke in. "When shall I 'ear the last of un? That man don't work iron like a natural man, 'e d'use magic. But 'e shan't 'ave the smith's job at Wheal Fortune."
> "Oh, won't 'e?"
> "I've 'Ector Bolitho's promise."
> "He might change 'is mind, 'e's a soft spot for Welland. While that man stays in Windfall, your job's not certain."
> "There's naught I can do about it."

In *Notes from the Country Club*, a novel about a battered woman coming to terms with the events that have brought her to prison, the writer Kim Wozencraft describes a conversation between a Latina and a WASP in the prison (the "country club" of the book's title). Wozencraft, author of the best-selling *Rush*, deliberately avoids trying to create accent artificially. The effectiveness of the piece is in the information conveyed and the careful choice of detail (using "gringa" and "gringita" for example, and the casual mention of the Mariel boat lift from Cuba) that allows us to fill in a lot of the gaps for ourselves.

> "Good move, gringa," she says. "I want so much to see the end of this flick."
>
> "Herlinda," I whisper, "how long have you been here?"
>
> "Let me see," she sighs. "It is fourteen months now."
>
> "In the States, I mean."
>
> "Since the boats," she says. She nods toward the table. "All of us together. Since Mariel."
>
> Coffee rouses herself to glare from her place on the other couch.
>
> "Hey," she whispers, "you bitches want to talk, go on down the hall. *Some* of us are trying to stay with the program here."
>
> Herlinda looks at sleeping Mrs. Palazzetti, then at me, and shrugs. I follow the clinking of her jewelry down A Hall, past Conchita, past the towel hanging over the window of Nina's door, and into 306.
>
> "We're not supposed to congregate in the room," I say, knowing this would be only my first offense. I would get away with a warning, which is why I'm willing to risk it.
>
> "Gringita," Herlinda laughs, "what are they going to do if they catch you? Put you in jail?"

How to convey an accent was a problem I gave some thought to in my novel *Werewolf*, which, despite its title, is actually a murder mystery set in the East End of London during the Blitz of World War II. Here's an example of how I tried to convey a cockney accent that's authentic and at the same time intelligible to Americans:

"Seen the papers this morning," Ethel Tanner asked.

The two policemen shook their heads . . . . The headline read, "Nazi Werewolf Terrorizes East End" . . . George showed the newspaper article to Fred Medford. "You should know better than to believe this load of old rubbish," he said to Mrs. Tanner. "It's worse than that one about them Jerries dropping plague rats on us."

"Oh, so that's what them little parachutes was for," Medford said."

"Get away with you, you foolish man!"

DC Williams, returning with the teas, overheard Medford and was suddenly caught by a violent coughing fit, nearly spilling the contents of the tray he was carrying.

In the final excerpt coming up, it doesn't take much to realize we are in Ireland on Christmas Day at the turn of the century, and to hear the brogues of the speakers. A *Portrait of the Artist as a Young Man* by James Joyce is arguably the most accessible piece of fiction written by one of this century's greatest writers of fiction. The book is a technically brilliant piece of biographical storytelling, and all serious fiction writers should read this novel. In all family gatherings, such as Thanksgiving, Christmas, Easter, birthday parties, and so forth, it seems there is always a point when a serious argument breaks out between people we love but don't see very often. We can probably all recall similar events, particularly from our childhood, when the grown-ups grew heated over things that made no real sense to us. Notice also the musical rhythm of the language and the dialogue, and the way it is paced. Joyce was an accomplished amateur musician, with a fine tenor voice. His musical ear can be heard clearly in the following example:

—That was a good answer our friend made to the canon. What? said Mr. Dedalus.

—I didn't think he had that much in him, said Mr. Casey.

—*I'll pay you your dues, father, when you cease turning the house of God into a pollingbooth.*

—A nice answer, said Dante, for any man calling himself a Catholic to give his priest.

—They have only themselves to blame, said Mr. Dedalus suavely. If they took a fool's advice they would confine their attention to religion.

—It is religion, Dante said. They are doing their duty in warning the people.

—We go to the house of God, Mr. Casey said, in all humility to pray to our Maker and not to hear election addresses.

—It is religion, Dante said again. They are right. They must direct their flocks.

—And preach politics from the altar, is it? asked Mr. Dedalus.

—Certainly, said Dante. It is a question of public morality. A priest would not be a priest if he did not tell his flock what is right and what is wrong.

Mrs. Dedalus laid down her knife and fork, saying,

—For pity's sake and for pity sake let us have no political discussion on this day of all days in the year.

—Quite right, ma'am, said Uncle Charles. Now, Simon, that's quite enough now. Not another word now.

—Yes, yes said Mr. Dedalus quickly.

He uncovered the dish boldly and said:

—Now then, who's for more turkey?

## 4.9    Exercises in Developing and Showing Character

- Make a list of half a dozen descriptive details to suggest a character for each of the following:

  1. Old age
  2. Young and married
  3. Adolescence
  4. A soldier
  5. A victim of violence
  6. Someone with a strong propensity for violence
  7. Someone drunk
  8. Someone who knows the answer to a question but is restrained from shouting out the answer until he or she is called upon.

- Now name a character within the first two sentences and then write short, succinct character sketches for all of the foregoing, picking only *three or four* details from each list to *show* us the character. Do not *tell* anything.

- Reread the synopsis of *Beauty and the Beast*, and come up with several character sketches for the main characters in one of the story variations you previously developed.

- Figure out what your main characters in the *Beauty and the Beast* story want. Now figure out what they fear. Who or what is standing in the way of their attaining what they want?

- Write a page of dialogue between the father and Beauty developing story and conflict without *telling* or explaining anything, and yet convey important information the reader needs to follow the story and learn about the character's personality.

- Without once lapsing into either cliché or bad taste, write the following scenes: (1) two children no older than thirteen deliberately murdering a younger child, (2) a rookie police officer discovering the body, and (3) a senior police officer, who is the father of boys the same age as the murderers, interviewing the culprits in a police station.

# 5

# Viewpoint:
# Whose Story Is It?

"The choice of the point(s) of view from which the story is told is arguably the most important single decision that the novelist has to make, for it fundamentally affects the way readers will respond, emotionally and morally, to the fictional characters and their actions."

*–David Lodge*

Point of view, or viewpoint, is a storytelling element that many writers—both published and unpublished—don't consider adequately. It's not enough to have figured out the plot and the characters in your story. You also need to think about *how best to tell this story.* Choosing a story's viewpoint focuses and shapes your work in a decisive way.

Selecting a viewpoint is a major challenge in storytelling. The problem is not just how best to convey all the information the reader needs in order to understand and enjoy the story, but how to do it with a minimum of dodging from one character's viewpoint to another's, and with little or no narrative exposition.

## 5.1   Avoid Too Many Points of View

Some writers find that, while they have concentrated on making sure they "show" and not "tell" their story, it still doesn't work because somehow the story has no coherence, or it's too long, dull, and obvious. Often, this problem is caused by telling the story from too many points of view. Using multiple viewpoints is a complex technique akin to juggling with sharp knives, and while it can be a feature of the best-selling blockbuster novel, invariably these successful novelists have practiced their craft on simpler stories first. James Clavell, for example, first wrote *King Rat*, a limited viewpoint, third-person novel, before publishing the expansive *Shogun*, which is told from multiple viewpoints.

What results from shifting from character to character within scenes and in successive scenes, if not done skillfully, is the sacrifice of character development to manipulative storytelling and predictable plotting. It is the mark of a lazy or unimaginative writer. When writers use multiple viewpoints poorly, readers have no idea how they should react to the people they meet in the story (Who is the hero and who is the villain?); and they become either bewildered or bored and put the story down, probably never to pick it up again.

Ideally, the best choice is to convey what's important to the reader from a single, unwavering viewpoint. Writing a novel this way can be difficult, but the more successful you are the stronger your fiction because readers have more opportunity to become emotionally involved in the story and care about what happens to its characters. Limiting the viewpoint forces you to focus on the important elements of storytelling, such as imagination and invention, and also forces you to discard a great deal of the extraneous material that insecurity about finishing a full-length novel manuscript causes you to use to pad your work.

In the short story in particular, the uniformity of point of view is of special importance. You just don't have the space to jump around too much, and you may well undermine the effectiveness of your story by trying.

## 5.2   Whose Eyes Are We Using?

Uniformity of both point of view and narrative voice reduces the chances of jerking the reader out of the fictive dream. As your storytelling skills increase (like a painter who becomes more and more confident with an increasing palette of colors), so you'll discover and invent tools, techniques, and solutions to increasingly complex technical problems that may arise with each story you create. Eventually you may become comfortable with using more than one point of view to tell a story, and the technique will succeed for you.

Point of view is about whose "eyes" we use to witness the action of the story. There are basically three ways to do this: first-person, third-person subjective, and third-person objective. In each case, the choice of viewpoint creates a deliberate *psychic distance* between the reader and the observer of events in the story. By this, I mean the writer's deliberate choice of how intimate and involved with the characters the reader should become.

## 5.3   First-Person Viewpoint

First-person is clearly the most intimate experience readers can have, because they can get inside a main character's head and become privy to all sorts of thoughts and feelings.

However, even first-person can create degrees of psychic distance. The "I" character can be the subject of the story (as in Scott Turow's *Presumed Innocent,* or *The Stranger* by Albert Camus), which is the closest we can get. The "I" character can also be narrating another character's story. Such is the case with Scout, the narrator of Harper Lee's *To Kill a Mockingbird,* who is really telling us Atticus's story, or the title character in E. L. Doctorow's *Billy Bathgate,* who, by telling us about his summer with the gangster Dutch Schultz, tells the gangster's story. One of the most famous novels using this point of view begins, "Call me Ishmael . . . ." (*Moby Dick*). A problem with first-person viewpoint, however, is that it locks you into one character's mind and therefore also generally limits you to one tone of voice throughout the story.

One of the reasons James Joyce's *A Portrait of the Artist as a Young Man* is such an important novel is that, not only does the central character change from the beginning of the story to the end, but the tone of the narrative voice changes with him. This is exceptionally difficult to do well, however, and even with *Portrait* . . . we are dealing with a third-person narrative, albeit one so intimate it might as well be first-person.

It's easy to confuse "Whose story is it?" with "Who is telling the story?" They are not the same thing. *To Kill a Mockingbird* is a great example of how this problem is handled successfully. So, too, are F. Scott Fitzgerald's *The Great Gatsby* and Oscar Hijuelos's Pulitzer Prize–winning *The Mambo Kings Play Songs of Love.* In each of these novels, a minor first-person character tells us a story about someone else so that in effect it allows the author a *limited* editorial comment on the action *through the eyes of the narrating character.*

First-person novels, while in many ways the most rewarding to read when they are written properly, are deceptively difficult to write. "I," the character narrating the story, and "I," the author writing the story, can become confused in the inexperienced writer's mind. The reader becomes equally confused, unable to connect with a weak or colorless narrating character. First-person is the only point of view, however, in which a narrating character can legitimately lie to readers without cheating them because they are forced to read between the lines to get to the truth. The author, therefore, must be particularly attentive to the way in which he or she objectively dramatizes and shows the right incidents to give readers the clues necessary to discover the truth of the story—which ultimately may contradict the fictional narrator's view of it.

Imagine, for example, a first-person narrator who tells the reader about a job interview. Let's assume she is an attractive housewife who lives in a trailer park.

I was really nervous, I mean really. I got Julie to pick up Adam from school, and watch him in case I was late back and waited in the dentist's outer office for what seemed like hours flipping through all these magazines I got no interest in reading. Except for maybe US and People, which I'd already read, anyway. My husband Joe and my Dad figure too much reading is bad for you. I guess they're right. Anyway, I could hear this drill whistling in fits and starts somewhere behind the counter, and there was all this quiet piped music from some light FM radio station or something. I tried not to bite my nails too much, you know, just neaten them up a bit with my teeth.

Finally, Dr. Wiseman comes out and takes me into his office. He was a young guy, about thirty or so I guess, dressed in like a doctor's white jacket, and I began wondering how I'd tell Joe I was working for this good looking young Jew dentist. He gets crazy when I even want to go over my friend Julie's house, and now he's out of work he's got even worse. But we need the money this job would bring in, 'cause his unemployment's almost run out and food stamps don't get us squat these days.

"So," Dr, Wiseman says from behind his desk, looking me up and down kind of like Joe used to when we was dating, "you want the receptionist's job. What experience have you had?" Well, there was a problem right there. I mean, I've been stuck at home looking after a kid for four years and never even finished high school. But I couldn't very well tell him that now, could I?

She describes the rest of the interview and the employer's promise to "get back to her next week." Next week arrives, and he puts her off for another week, but mentions he'd like to meet her after work sometime for a drink—another informal interview. It becomes clear to the reader that the employer is stringing along the young woman, who is more than a little naïve, if not a little slow, and that he has no intention of giving her the job. What's more, if she persists, she could get into trouble if her husband finds out what's going on. The dentist, it seems, may have a devious reason for simply not telling the narrator he's hired someone else. But, if the narrator continues to maintain to readers that she is sure she will get the job soon and starts to plan around it, she is lying to them, albeit also lying to herself.

The deception comes from the *character's interpretation* of scenes that are objectively drawn. This juxtaposition of interpretation and observation can reveal a character's personality while also propelling the story forward.

The fabric of the story takes shape from the threads this narrative is starting to weave. This comes back to the need to pose questions and then answer them in dramatic form. What does the dentist want from her? What will happen if Joe finds out she's having secret meetings with the dentist? Or that she's gone looking for a job in the first place? How will she get out of the hole she is beginning to dig for herself? What is this story about? A young woman's quest for freedom from a confining life? Is this a coming-of-age story? The possibilities are many.

Having a character lie to readers is a subtle technique, one that is difficult to pull off. It's only worth using if the character's self-delusion and its eventual exposure will in some way influence the story's climax. As an exercise, write a short story with an ending in which a self-deceiving narrator is forced to confront the truth about his or her deceptions.

What if we took another viewpoint to tell this story of the dentist and the young woman? If the narrator is Julie, the friend, the narrative takes a different tone.

> I knew there was a problem the moment Bobby Sue told me about the interview. I mean, it took two years just for her to, like, convince her husband, Joe, to let her learn how to drive. When she got back from this interview she was so excited, and told me about this good-looking young dentist who was going to hire her as his receptionist. I mean, Joe wasn't going to like that one little bit. I just knew she was heading for trouble.

Another problem arises when writing a first-person novel: The narrator may end up *telling* readers information that might be more effective if shown in a dramatic scene. As a result, the character never really develops as fully as he or she should, but comes across as somewhat two-dimensional. A good way to detect whether this is a problem in your story is to start rewriting it in the third-person to see whether you are telling too much, and showing too little.

In the first of the above examples, if you were to rewrite it in the third-person, which information would you dramatize? We know that Bobby Sue left her friend Julie's house, after arranging for Julie to look after Adam. But dramatizing that scene really doesn't take us very far. Bobby Sue spent a long time waiting for the dentist, Dr. Wiseman, to come out and interview her. Perhaps that should be dramatized? The problem is that it's a static scene with little action. So, in a third-person narrative, we would want to start the scene where the action really starts, when Bobby Sue and Dr. Wiseman meet.

The moment Bobby Sue laid eyes on Dr. Wiseman, she knew her life was about to change. The dentist crossed the room, and shook her hand, then ushered her down the thick carpeted hallway into his office and waved her into the chair across the desk from his own. He sat back, and turned sideways for a moment to offer his profile. Bobby Sue wondered whether everyone felt as weak-kneed as she did the first time they saw his suntanned Mediterranean features.

Using this third-person narrative, the information about Bobby Sue's background, her jealous, overprotective husband, the fact that she hasn't ever really worked at a job since leaving school, that she has a four-year-old son, must all be dramatized later for best effect. Part of that information can be imparted in a scene with Julie after Bobby Sue returns from the interview. *"How did it go?" Julie asked,* would be the obvious beginning to that scene, followed soon after by, *"How are you going to break the news to Joe?"* as the next important line, after Bobby Sue tells Julie she is sure she has the job.

The situation with the husband, in particular, which should be alluded to at first and then developed as a confrontational scene or series of scenes, will obviously vary in the way you dramatize it according to the point of view you've chosen. This mention of problems with Joe, as I've illustrated, can't be easily foreshadowed at the onset of a third-person narrative. It can be, however, if you use the first-person. Bobby Sue's reply to Julie's question, rather than something expository such as, *"Oh, I know how jealous Joe gets, and I know he doesn't want me to work but he'll come round,"* should be something more true to life, such as a simple anguished, *"I don't know."*

All of the above, of course, is contingent on the *kind* of character we create in Bobby Sue; that is, a young woman whose story is about how she finds the necessary moxie to escape a domineering and potentially abusive husband. The climax of the story will be what happens between Bobby Sue and the dentist. The fact that she has gone for the interview is her first sign of independent action and therefore where the story should start.

You'll probably have noticed that, structurally, third-person narratives are inherently more cinematic than first-person. First-person narratives, however, also need a cinematic quality to be effective, but you can move the action along a little faster. There is a difference, for example, between foreshadowing something, ("How are you going to break the news to Joe?"), and telling us ("Oh, I know how jealous he gets . . .").

In the case of a thriller written in the first-person, the reader knows that the narrator can't perish (*Falling Angel* by William Hjortsberg is a story where this isn't the case) and therefore is never really in serious danger, which dulls the story's impact. One of the reasons Scott Turow's *Presumed Innocent* is so engaging is that the author deliberately plays with the reader by raising exactly this question: Did this first-person narrator do it or didn't he? Agatha Christie, while not a great stylist, used the same viewpoint technique to great effect in *The Murder of Roger Ackroyd*.

A particularly subtle consideration of first-person narrative that isn't given adequate consideration by writers is the question, Who's the audience for this first-person narrative? Is it the reader, or another character in the story? Can the fact that it is a first-person story play a part in shaping the ending in some way? Can we trust what we are being told? Is the story a confession, or something that, once recounted, will round off the story beyond the simple narrative of events? Pierre Boule's *Monkey Planet*, which became the basis for the movie *Planet of the Apes* (he also wrote *The Bridge Over the River Kwai*), cleverly uses this narrative technique.

## 5.4  Second-Person Viewpoint

One or two people will bravely try second-person ("you"), but this viewpoint isn't often successful unless it's used for a specific reason. A debatably successful example was Jay McInerny's best-selling *Bright Lights, Big City*. More often than not, writers use second-person merely to attract attention, and it becomes an irritating affectation. The most obvious problem with second-person is that readers become confused about who is telling the story and who the story is really about. Instead of drawing readers into a story in a way that evokes an everyman feel, second-person viewpoint can quickly have the opposite effect and, instead, cause readers to be held at arm's length from any emotional involvement with the story or its characters.

It has been used to some effect in some feminist-inspired literature, however, particularly stories that deal with the brutalizing of women. The "you" voice becomes easily identifiable to women, who can empathize with the character and recognize the situations as familiar, while for many men the point of view is effective for its ability to make them rethink situations or events from a perspective they hadn't previously considered.

> You just know that you have to do something. Things can't keep on the way they've been going. If not for your sake, then at least for the children's you know it's time to get away from him. If he were to put you in the hospital once more, what would be your chances of surviving? Part of you dismisses this sort of thinking as melodramatic nonsense—but part of you knows his drinking is getting worse, and the more he drinks the angrier he gets, it seems. How much longer will it be before he does something you will both regret?

## 5.5   Third-Person Objective Viewpoint

The most common viewpoint used in storytelling is third-person. Here again, you can choose the degree of reader involvement with the story by deciding to use third-person objective or omniscient (the author is god and knows everybody's thoughts and feelings) or third-person subjective (readers are looking over the shoulder of a character and are privy to some of that character's thoughts and feelings. "I" has essentially become "he" or "she").

Third-person objective sets the reader at the greatest distance from the story. It is as though the reader is on top of a cloud, floating over the action of the story while the characters scurry about their business below. It was a common narrative form in the nineteenth-century and was often accompanied by a strong authorial presence (for example, "Listen, dear reader, while I tell you about . . .") but has largely fallen out of favor. At first glance it would seem a wonderful way to tell a story, for the author can know and tell everything without worrying about rules or limitations, but it has serious drawbacks. One of the most important is that it is a hard technique to control and gives readers no real touchstone for identifying with the characters, and thus no way of understanding the story. With third-person objective, there are no guidelines—and too many choices.

The weaknesses of third-person objective are also its advantages: It gives you the most range and freedom, allowing for the use of different narrative voices; it helps to fill in background material; it offers ways to comment on the action, or draw back and vanish from view as an intense scene unfolds. But inexperienced writers who may not yet have mastered these narrative tools can end up dizzying and distracting readers, not edifying and entertaining them.

Just because you *can* go into every character's head doesn't mean you should. If you feel you must tell your story by jumping from character to character, you probably haven't thought enough about the best way to dramatize it. Furthermore, the narrator in third-person objective fiction becomes a persona of the author, and if you're not careful you can become an obtrusive and annoying distraction for the reader as the tale unfolds. The most fruitful way to use third-person objective nowadays is probably in comedy or satire.

> Little did the mayor know that while he was on his way to work his wife was once again "entertaining" the grocery boy while the boy's sister sat in a tree outside the bedroom window with a camera and a tape recorder recording everything that went on between the clandestine lovers.

As the upcoming excerpt reveals, Jane Austen used this viewpoint in *Pride and Prejudice* in 1813. This is definitely third-person objective because the author is clearly present as storyteller. What makes this such an interesting example, however, is that in 1993 there were no less than two "sequels" to this book published by contemporary writers. The contemporary books, *Pemberley: Or Pride and Prejudice Continued* by Emma Tennant and *Presumption* by Julia Barrett, became known in the publishing industry as the "Jane Wars."

> . . . turning around [Mr. Darcy] looked for a moment at Elizabeth, till catching her eye, he withdrew his own and coldly said, "She is tolerable, but not handsome enough to tempt *me*; and I am in no humor at present to give consequence to young ladies who are slighted by other men. You had better return to your partner and enjoy her smiles, for you are wasting your time with me."
> Mr. Bingley followed his advice. Mr. Darcy walked off; and Elizabeth remained with no very cordial feelings to-

wards him. She told the story, however, with great spirit among her friends; for she had a lively, playful disposition, which delighted in anything ridiculous.

The evening altogether passed off pleasantly to the whole family. Mrs. Bennett had seen her eldest daughter much admired by the Netherfield party. Mr. Bingley had danced with her twice, and she had been distinguished by her sisters. Jane was as much gratified by this as her mother could be, though in a quieter way.

This is clearly a nineteenth-century tone of voice, and the style would probably only work in a modern novel if you were trying to create a period piece. Jane Austen was one of the first English novelists, male or female, to fully appreciate the importance of point of view in giving the reader close participation in a story. *Pride and Prejudice* works largely because we experience it through Elizabeth's viewpoint. In fact, it is a tribute to Austen's skill as a novelist that, though we may soon suspect that Darcy is in love with Elizabeth, even perceiving the book from her point of view we don't know that Elizabeth is in love with Darcy for a while because of the way Austen manipulates the point of view.

## 5.6 Third-Person Subjective Viewpoint

Most novels by beginning writers are probably best told in third-person subjective. However, many of the problems associated with first-person come into play here, too. The biggest drawback with either third-person subjective or first-person point of view is that, if your book is to obey its own rules, logically there are going to be things that the reader may need to know to make the story work—things that the central character must not or cannot know. The writer's challenge is to present this information to the reader while keeping it from the character at this point in the story.

There is no simple solution to this challenge. There are obvious and rather clichéd solutions, such as finding a diary or letter or eavesdropping on other characters as they discuss the information. This problem creates much greater difficulties in first-person stories than it does in novels written in third-person subjective, though. The main advantage of third-person subjective over first-person is that, when all else fails, you can shift viewpoints as needed without disturbing the fictive dream and distracting the reader from the story. The best place to first shift viewpoint, however, is after the character with the new viewpoint has already been introduced to the reader, ideally by the main viewpoint character.

The choice of point of view will also affect your selection of narrative style. Will it be formal, colloquial, or in dialect? Will the extent and range of the vocabulary you use be in keeping with the viewpoint? The problems here center mainly on overwriting and readability. The beginning writer with a keen ear for dialect or the colloquial may try to capture as accurately as possible what she knows to be a true representation of a character's accent or way of talking. Alas, as I discussed in Chapter 4, while the representation may be accurate, when overdone it is often unintelligible to and unreadable by the majority. Dialect and obscure colloquialisms are like spices in cooking: A little goes a very long way.

As an exercise, write a 200-word piece from the point of view of an intelligent character who deliberately acts and talks like a hick. Do not explain or "tell" the reader anything.

Point of view determines how you will comment on the characters and unfold the action through the eyes of one or more characters. Using a coarse voice to tell the story of *Beauty and the Beast,* for example, offers a challenge that can really only be met by finding a brutish character through whom you would tell the tale. (Read John Gardner's novel *Grendel* to see how this can be done effectively.)

For many stories, particularly those written in third-person, a slightly formal, elegant narrative voice works well as a simple setting for characters who have eccentric or idiosyncratic ways of speaking. When the narrative voice and the characterization do not fight for the reader's attention, the characterizations take on a "three-dimensional" quality that makes the best novels enviably well written. A gracefully written third-person narrative lets you create clear but "invisible" prose that adds to a reader's sense of involvement in the story. Amy Tan's *The Joy Luck Club* is a good example of this type of writing, as is much of the work of Toni Morrison, John le Carré and Doris Lessing.

First-person or third-person subjective viewpoints give an immediacy to a story that virtually no other voice can duplicate as effectively. For example, consider this opening sentence from the novel *Snakes in the Garden* by L. S. Whiteley:

The night they found Grandfather, barefoot, checkbook in hand, sprawled on the ground in one of the back pastures with two bullet holes in the back of his skull, I was in bed with my business partner's wife.

Had this been written in the third-person, while still effective, it would clearly have lost some of its impact. Telling something bad about a character is less effective than having a character admit what he's done, for it reduces confession to gossip. I include the foregoing excerpt because it was precisely the appealing immediacy of both the point-of-view character and the narrative voice of the novel that convinced me as a publishing house editor to publish this book, which I did to some critical success.

I've said it before, but it bears repeating: Avoid the common mistake writers make in trying to switch from first-person to third and back again. Except in the case of monologues or diaries and letters, this jerks readers out of the fictive dream and draws their attention to the fact that an author is present. It is like viewing a scene through a camera lens that keeps zooming from closeup to long shot while someone is whispering distractingly in your ear. It is, at the least, disorienting.

Consider the following six examples written from three different viewpoints, thinking not just about third- and first-person, but also about the effectiveness of the narrative (i.e., psychic) distance from the reader as the lens draws a little closer and the reader's emotional involvement becomes more intense with each example:

Third-Person Objective

1. A rich merchant and his family fell upon hard times and were forced to abandon their sumptuous mansion for a small cottage and meager lifestyle in the forest.

One day, news came that one of the merchant's ships may have survived the storm that destroyed his fleet and his fortune.

2. Monsieur Dumont's daughters no longer found life as pleasant as it had been, and he blamed himself for that. Ever since losing the family fortune, he had sunk into a depression that deepened with every week that went by without a solution to his problem.

When the Dumonts had been forced to sell their house, it affected Rose, the eldest, particularly hard. She had grown angry at her useless father and parasitic siblings, and the anger only grew worse with each day she had to spend in the filthy hovel they now called home. Her sister Beatrice had become equally bad tempered, for the young men who had once courted her no longer bothered to come around.

Only the youngest, whose nickname was Beauty, seemed to cope with the devastating bad luck they had all suffered.

Third-Person Subjective

3. George Dumont hated the pass he had come to: in one fateful afternoon, all his wealth had disappeared like so much sand through his fingers. That mousy-faced clod, Rambeau, had burst into the busy counting-house and announced in a voice too loud that Monsieur's ships were "lost, lost," all the while wringing his hands and pulling his hair. "What are we to do?" he wailed. M. Dumont wished the fool would just be silent so that he could think. Yet he said nothing, bearing the news stoically for the sake of appearances in front of his staff and customers, allowing the chief clerk to hustle the hysterical Rambeau into a back room and out of the public eye.

4. *Mon Dieu*, how she hated all this squabbling. It was driving her crazy. It had started even before Papa's ships had been lost at sea, but since then things had gotten worse. The family had gone from riches to rags almost overnight, it seemed to Beauty, but it was the bickering and fighting among her brothers and sisters that upset her the most. She tried hard to remember what her poor dead mama had told her about respecting her elders and being ladylike and above the common fray; but stuck as she was in such a small, damp, crowded cottage after living in a huge mansion for as long as she could remember, it was hard to remain calm and pleasant. What she really felt like doing was screaming at everyone to stop being so selfish and helpless. They were all like a bunch of fish flopping about on the river bank. It wasn't Papa's fault. He hadn't caused that stupid storm!

First Person

5. I never thought that M. Dumont would survive the loss of those ships and his fortune, but to my surprise he had.

Other men in his position would have succumbed to the temptation to put a pistol ball into their temple rather than endure the lasting shame and ignominy that was bound to follow such ruin. In the morning he had gone to work a respected and important member of the Merchant's Guild, and by evening he was a shattered man and a social outcast. What was worse, as far as I was concerned, was that along with M. Dumont's vanishing fortune had gone any hopes I had of marrying his middle daughter, Beatrice. Once my father had discovered the girl no longer had a dowry or a position in society, he quickly made his disapproval known to me. Such a match would be out of the question for the son of an important Alderman such as himself, even if the girl in question was one of the three most beautiful in town. And what was I to do, disobey my father for the love of a girl I could not possibly hope to support without his help? The situation seemed both hopeless and desperate as I rode over to M. Dumont's cottage to console with Beatrice, perhaps for the last time.

6. It was getting well into the morning when I looked up from hanging out the laundry on the new clothesline my brother Arnaud had rigged up, and saw the bedraggled figure of Papa ride up the forest trail to the cottage. The horse looked almost as worse for wear after the terrible storm we had suffered last night as its ashen-faced rider did, and I knew at once, despite the red rose poking from within the folds of his great coat, things had not gone well in his efforts to prevail in the teeth of the disaster that had befallen his business—and our family.

Daniel Keyes's wonderful, prize-winning story "Flowers for Algernon" (I recommend reading the short story first rather than the novel he later developed from it) is a terrific example of the effectiveness of using a correctly chosen point of view. Told in the form of diary entries, it is the story of a medical experiment made on a retarded man to make him more intelligent. As the story progresses, we see the increase in the main character's intelligence as much from the way the piece is written as the character's insights into his situation.

While technical demands differ when shifting between short-story and novel writing, the one technique that is largely common to both forms of storytelling is the choice and effectiveness of viewpoint. Writing short stories is a great way to practice and experiment with point of view. It is an interesting exercise to write half a dozen letters no longer than, say, 1,500 words from different characters to friends or relatives about events in their lives. If you're not sure how to do this, try writing the letter as you would write it, then construct a character, based perhaps on a friend of someone you know well, and imagine how they would have written about the *same* subject. If you need some suggestions for topics, try the following: surviving an earthquake, an armed robbery in a subway car, meeting a strange man in a video store, the first time the writer went to night school, winning a ten-pin bowling competition, a child or adolescent at boarding school for the first time, and so on. The point is not just to recount the event or scene, which can be quite simple, but to do so through the eyes of a *character*. The same event means different things to different people. How different, and perhaps insufferable, the Sherlock Holmes stories would have been if Holmes had been the narrator, not John Watson. You can perhaps begin to see, especially if you do the above exercise, how the choice of viewpoint is vital in recounting your story, be it short or long.

Point of view demands inventiveness from the writer, but the rewards for hard work can be many and are worth the effort writers put into thinking out and properly planning their stories. Only experimentation and experience can really teach you which point of view and narrative style is appropriate, and when. Once again, the rule of thumb is: If in doubt, keep it simple.

## 5.7   Exercises in Point of View

- Write a page in the first-person assuming the viewpoint of someone of the opposite sex, the idea being to try to get "under their skin," if only briefly.

- Imagine a stone-age man who has spent his life just struggling to stay alive. During the hunt one day his oldest son is seriously injured and brought back to camp. That night the old man looks up and studies the starry heavens for the first time. Without mentioning or alluding to the man, the son, the injury, or any other character, write a fifty-word description of the old man's world from his viewpoint. (This is another exercise in description as a function of character. It should, ideally, illuminate the character without being expository.)

- Having completed the foregoing exercise, write a 250-word description of the same world, from the point of view of the son, in either first or third person.

- Now write the scene from the third-person viewpoint of either the injured man's wife or mother and then write it in a first-person viewpoint from the same character's point of view.

- Write a short story in which the character lies to the reader, but in the end is forced to admit that he (or she) has been lying.

- Imagine a memorable incident that happened in a character's childhood. Describe that incident from the point of view of the child. Then write about the same incident from the point of view of the child as a much older person, recollecting with adult experiences and maturity.

# 6

# Pacing of Information: Pulling the Rabbit out of the Hat

"Sit down and put down everything that comes into your head and then you're a writer. But an author is one who can judge his own stuff's worth, without pity, and destroy most of it."

—Colette

If there is a "trick" to writing good fiction, it is striking a balance between keeping the characters growing and their dilemmas interesting, while at the same time revealing just enough plot to make what is happening intelligible. Too much plot and character information destroys suspense and produces turgid prose; too little such information makes your story bewildering.

Feeding the reader just the right amount of these facts is called *pacing of information*. It concerns how you present *all* the information readers will need to make sense of your story. At its simplest, pacing of information breaks down into three components: *what* the reader is told; *when* the reader is told these facts; and *how* the reader is told this information.

As I mentioned in Chapter 4, plot is what characters do

next. If you prepare a story synopsis and character notes, by the time you come to write your novel or short story you should have a good idea of the main points of your story's progress from beginning to end and the kinds of characters who will take part in it. What you should now be thinking about is *how* something is going to happen on the page, not *what* is going to happen, which you should already know at least broadly.

The best way to dramatize important story information is to concentrate on developing true-to-life characters. By writing fiction this way, you distract readers from thinking about a story's *plot* by engrossing them in the lives of your *characters*. In the best fiction the two are essentially the same—"Character is plot," said Henry James. Correct pacing of information is the literary equivalent of the magician waving his right hand (character development) to distract us from watching his left hand (plot development), which is vital in the process of producing a live rabbit (the story) from a hat.

## 6.1   How Should I Dramatize My Story?

At its heart, pacing of information requires the writer to develop an instinct for what makes successful drama. The question you should always ask yourself is: "What is the best way to dramatize my story?"

This assumes a writer understands the difference between good drama and melodrama. Melodrama is broadly defined as fiction that is histrionically sensational, artificially and heavily loaded with suspense, oversentimentalized in episode and characterization, and usually arrives at a forced happy ending. Almost any TV soap opera can serve as an example of melodrama, as can a great deal of early pulp fiction.

## 6.2 Show, Don't Tell–2

Good drama, on the other hand, can be broadly defined as a character or characters moving from one dramatized conflict or dilemma to another until the resolution of the story is reached. At its most extreme, this sort of storytelling is what drives the Indiana Jones-type of story. If there is one clearly positive influence on modern fiction that *good* film-making and playwriting has had (I mean by that a combination of strong writing, directing, and acting), it is to make writers instinctively aware of the importance of *dramatization* as opposed to reportage. In other words, *show* don't *tell*.

Writing a synopsis *before* you write your story is important because it allows you to focus on how best, that is how subtly and entertainingly, you can convey story information to the reader. Freed of the need to figure out the basics of the plot (which you should have already drawn broadly), you can concentrate on what really makes a good story: strong character ization. You already know *where* you want your characters to end up, so, during the first draft phase of writing, you are figuring out how best to get them there.

A story told by Alfred Hitchcock concerned the nature of good suspense: Two men sit at a cafe table discussing baseball. Suddenly, the table explodes, killing them. Reactions of shock and horror ensue from the audience—but, also, a feeling they have been somehow cheated. Where did that bomb come from?

What if, however, we first saw a man place a bomb under the table? Our two protagonists now arrive and begin talking about baseball. Meanwhile, the audience is in suspense wondering when the bomb under the table will go off. The explosion, when it comes, is almost a relief from the growing tension of the scene. Frederick Forsythe's *Day of the Jackal* is a very good example of this type of suspense writing. We know the assassin sent to kill President De Gaulle will fail. The suspense comes in waiting to see how far this extremely resourceful killer will get before he is stopped, and how he is stopped. Forsythe milks this suspense right up to the last few pages.

## 6.3   When and How to Reveal the Right Detail

Proper pacing of information is about choosing the right detail and deciding when and how to reveal it. Details in fiction are not just ornaments; they should be catalysts for action and for emotional drama. For example, if a character were to pick up a book that is, in some fashion, important to the story, you should describe it—is it leather bound, worn from too much reading, a hardcover novel, a paperback, a coffee-table type?— and also describe how the character is holding the book. What is the character's reaction to this object? Is it a diary? Should the character be in possession of the book in the first place and be struggling with himself over whether to read it? The book no longer becomes just a book, but a means of revealing the possibilities of character. Almost certainly, the book should show up again in the story.

Every time you create a detail that has "life" and potential, such as the book, you give yourself the chance to reshape the fictive world you are creating. It is important then, to be conscious of the details you are inventing. Once an object has been injected into a story, that object can become unpredictable. That unpredictability offers you a means of exploring the world of your story.

Once the object is present it can be made to disappear, and its vanishing will have impact because its earlier presence was so clearly felt. The object becomes a means of exploring and probing the hidden nooks and crannies of your story's world. If it is a detective story then perhaps that lace handkerchief with lipstick marks on it may tell us something important?

Here are the opening paragraphs of William Golding's classic novel, *Lord of the Flies*. They comprise a great example of storytelling through a precise yet casually observed choice of detail:

The boy with fair hair lowered himself down the last few feet of rock and began to pick his way toward the lagoon. Though he had taken off his school sweater and trailed it now from one hand, his grey shirt stuck to him and his hair was plastered to his forehead. All round him the long scar smashed into the jungle was a bath of heat. He was clambering heavily among the creepers and broken trunks when a bird, a vision of red and yellow, flashed upwards with a witch-like cry; and this cry was echoed by another.

"Hi!" it said, "Wait a minute!"

The undergrowth at the side of the scar was shaken and a multitude of raindrops fell pattering.

"Wait a minute," the voice said. "I got caught up."

The fair boy stopped and jerked his stockings with an automatic gesture that made the jungle seem for a moment like the Home Counties.

Here is how the pacing of information in the foregoing passage can be broken down. Most obviously, we are faced with fish out of water—English schoolboys (one has "taken off his school sweater" and jerks "his stockings with an automatic gesture that made the jungle seem for a moment like the Home Counties"), on a tropical island (He "began to pick his way toward the lagoon."). There has been some sort of disaster ("the long scar *smashed* into the jungle"), and we are reminded of *Robinson Crusoe* and *The Swiss Family Robinson*, which are both popular young-adult castaway adventure stories. It's likely these boys have quite recently become castaways since they are still in their school uniforms. They haven't yet become comfortable with the absence of adult authority and rules and are still following them by wearing clothing much too warm for the changed climate they are now in. Their uniforms, in fact, are also a symbol of civilization, and casting off their uniforms will be a first step in casting off the restraints of civilization, which is a theme of the novel. In general, the boys' situation is obviously serious and they will need to find a way to survive quickly.

I am really only touching the surface of what is implied by the choice of detail here. Golding's book is a terrifically subtle example of great storytelling. In this opening passage the author gives us strong visual images that do exactly what good drama (according to Aristotle) should do:

1. Define character

2. Create atmosphere, and

3. Advance the action

## 6.4    Hook the Reader, Don't Just Set the Scene

A common fault of inexperienced writers is to load the beginning of the story with boring and meaningless biographical detail about characters and turgid narrative description, believing that it is important to first "set the scene" rather than immediately draw readers into the story. A character's background is meaningless unless it has a direct bearing on the story. If the background information is important, find a way to dramatize it. In a novel in particular, you have plenty of room to do so. There's no need to do it at the beginning.

The reader doesn't necessarily need to know all the biographical details you have worked out for your character. The purpose of figuring out background details and doing other such preparation is to help you fully envision character and scene when you sit down to write. Portray only what will effect the development of the story. Ask yourself, "If I tell the reader this fact, will it advance the storyline in some way?"

Another common problem occurs when a writer decides that starting with a bang really means that, and so begins a story with an explosion or action scene that has nothing to do with the rest of the story, in the forlorn hope that the action alone is enough to hook a reader's interest. The reader spends most of the book trying to figure out how the opening scene connects with the story and feels cheated when she reaches the end and discovers that it doesn't.

## 6.5   How to Create and Solve Storytelling Puzzles

Writing a story has a great deal in common with making and solving puzzles. Here are the general rules you should follow to solve your puzzle:

1. Follow the synopsis, which gives you the bare bones of what is going to happen and some suggestions as to why.

2. Take account of character sketches you've worked out, particularly for your central character, to give you some idea of who these events are going to happen to, how the characters are going to react to them, and, again, why.

3. Consider unity of viewpoint, which will determine how readers are going to view the action of the story, that is, who is telling the story and who the story is about (not necessarily the same things).

4. *Now*, within these broad guidelines, figure out how to create a scene that will both advance the plot and at the

same time develop the reader's emotional involvement with the characters—not an easy task.

Obviously, every scene's construction/creation problem is unique because the various factors involved in each scene in every story are different. What we are discussing here, in a sense, is how to train one's instinct for the dramatic. How can you tell what is important and what is of less consequence? There is no simple answer to that question.

As a test, ask yourself: If a detail or piece of information must be in my story, how can I find a way to dramatize it most effectively? What will be the impact, the implications of focusing on this detail? If the detail doesn't have a function in the story, why am I wasting the reader's time with it?

## 6.6  Writing Is like Carpentry

Learning how to correctly pace the important information in a story is the literary equivalent of a carpenter learning about different types of wood, how to cut joints properly, when to screw, when to nail, when to glue to create firmly built objects of strength and beauty. While this seems a very mechanical approach, in fact, the more experienced you become as a storyteller, the more you increase your judgment and instinct about what is dramatically sound, and the more intuitive your creativity becomes.

Pacing-of-information problems often stand out when you reach the rewrite or second-draft stage of a novel. After you've put the manuscript aside for a while, you forget precisely what you *intended* to write, and then you can deal more objectively with what you *actually* wrote. By blocking out the important points the story takes from A (the beginning) to Z (the ending), you can begin to see whether a particular scene works or even if it is needed, or whether you have too many characters and are thus diluting the drama. By reconsidering decisions about motivation and dramatization, you can concentrate on what to *leave out* or condense in order to give your story maximum impact.

This presupposes that you have sufficient command of your ego and enough writing experience to acknowledge there's a problem that needs fixing. Go through a first draft of almost any fiction writer's manuscript, and it's easy to make such margin comments as: *This scene drags, cut it*; *What is the motivation here?*; *Rewrite this as indirect narrative*; *Dramatize this!*; *Prose is awkward, rewrite*; *How could he know this?*; *Clumsy, awkward*, and so on.

## 6.7   *Know Your Ending*

So, how do we go about solving such problems? First, think about the *purpose* of the scene, that is, its mechanical function within the story. How does it advance the plot?

Second, *know your ending*. Only if you know where you are going can you successfully plot a route, via a series of connected dramatic scenes, to get there. This route is the thread or backbone that holds these scenes together.

Like moviemaking, modern storytelling involves linking a series of scenes or set pieces that propel the story forward. The way to best dramatize each scene is a problem you must solve in order to advance the story in the most elegantly inventive and credible manner. The prize for succeeding is a gracefully told and absorbing story. Failure means that you lose your reader's interest, and probably your chance to get published. A novel, in particular, is not told in a straight line, but as a series of linked circles foreshadowing or developing each other.

The canny writer manages to give us the information needed to understand the story and character and also *subtly* lay the groundwork for what is coming next. There is an inevitability about storytelling (in hindsight, for the reader) that should not be obvious. It's worth emphasizing that readers should reach the end of a story saying to themselves: "Why didn't I think of that?" not, "Where did that come from?"

# 7

# Motivation and Time Shifting

"The act of writing requires a constant plunging back into the shadows of the past where time hovers ghostlike."

*–Ralph Ellison*

Pacing of information, character motivation, and time shifting are intertwined. Motivation is concerned with *why* your characters act as they do and the best way of establishing the answer to that question is by showing it. If readers come to trust you as a storyteller—and this means that *everything* in your story is there for a purpose and isn't just window dressing—then readers quickly get the idea that even casual information in a scene will turn out to be important. Not only will you keep them turning the pages to find out how the information is relevant to the story's resolution, but they will make connections you want them to make without your having to comment or editorialize on the action.

For example, note in the following passage how Anne Tyler ends Chapter 1 of *Saint Maybe*. It is 1965, and seventeen-year-old Ian Bedloe has just gone up to his room after telling his older brother, Danny, that Danny's wife is being unfaithful:

In the street below, an engine roared up. What the hell? [Ian] drew aside the curtain and peered out. It was Danny's Chevy, all right. The headlights were two yellow ribbons swinging away from the curb. The car took off abruptly, peeling rubber. Ian dropped the curtain. He turned to confront himself in the mirror.

Near the stone wall at the end of the block the brakes should have squealed, but instead the roaring sound grew louder. It grew until something had to happen, and then there was a gigantic, explosive, complicated crash and then a delicate tinkle and then silence. Ian went on staring into his own eyes. He couldn't seem to look away. He couldn't even blink, couldn't move, because once he moved then time would start rolling forward again, and he already knew that nothing in his life would ever be the same again.

This tragic event transforms Ian's life. Gradually, we learn that Ian blames himself for Danny's "accidental" death, and that he has a secret guilt. Tyler's carefully paced revelations of what motivates Ian are what makes this novel so effective and entertaining.

Sometimes you can establish a character's motivation directly by dramatizing it through his words and deeds. At other times it must be done indirectly ("It looked like . . . ," or "John speculated that . . ."). *When* you tell and *how* you tell this character information is important to the success of the story.

Here's how Doris Lessing tackles the problem in *The Fifth Child*, a brilliant, short novel that defies the oversimplifications or pat analyses often applied to fiction. It's the story of how a liberal, loving English couple deal with the moral and ethical problems brought about by the birth of their fifth child, Ben, a sort of "cuckoo child." From the beginning, he is totally abnormal by society's standards. Here, early in the book, mother and child have just come home from the hospital. The choice of detail in the scene, and the scene itself, clearly foreshadow the problems that lie ahead, providing motivation for a great deal of what will follow:

> That night, in the connubial bedroom, [Harriet] sat up against a stack of pillows, nursing the baby. David was watching.
>
> Ben sucked so strongly that he emptied the first breast in less than a minute. Always, when a breast was nearly empty, he ground his gums together, and so she had to snatch him away before he could begin. It looked as if she were unkindly depriving him of the breast, and she heard David's breathing change. Ben roared with rage, fastened like a leech to the other nipple, and sucked so hard she felt that her whole breast was disappearing down his throat. This time, she left him on the nipple until he ground his gums hard together and she cried out pulling him away.
>
> "He's extraordinary," said David, giving her the support she needed.
>
> "Yes, he is, he's absolutely not ordinary."
>
> "But he's all right, he's just . . ."
>
> "A normal healthy fine baby," said Harriet, bitter, quoting the hospital.
>
> David was silent: it was this anger, this bitterness in her that he could not handle.

## 7.1 Transitions of Time–1

Motivation, by definition, implies that there was either an event in the past that is causing the characters to act as they are now, or a current ambition or fear that will shape how they act in the future. How best do you dramatize this information?

This question leads to the problem of how to deal with passages of time within a story, whether they are flashbacks or

flashforwards. Because you've plotted your story in a chronological order does not necessarily mean that you should tell it
that way. *What* the story is (i.e., the synopsis), and *how* you
dramatize it are different things.

We are also talking, partly, about transitions, or how to link
scenes. The best writers disclose story information through
dramatized scenes like a strip-tease artist taking off her clothes:
Just enough is revealed at any one time to hold the reader's
interest until the final naked revelation.

Generally, if a scene introduces important new information
it should be dramatized as *direct narrative*. The scenes written
this way will make up the main body of the "movie" in your
head that you're committing to paper.

Passages of time or events of secondary importance to the
story's development can be written as narrative bridges or
transitional passages (*indirect narrative*) in the same way that
dialogue can be written as direct or indirect speech.

Let's suppose, in the following example, we have a lot of new
and important information the reader hasn't seen before. The
scene is written in a dramatized, or direct narrative, form.

## 7.1.1   Direct Narrative

The snow lay on the forest floor like a pearl carpet, ob-
scuring whatever path lay beneath. Beauty glanced at her
father, lost in his thoughts, and wrapped her cloak tighter
to protect herself from the bite in the chill air. This was a
part of the forest she had never visited before, the trees
soot-colored and broad as a man with his arms thrown
wide. They stood together so thickly that the bare mass
of branches towering above created a permanent dusk.
Beauty was certain some enchantment possessed the
horses, for they knew exactly where to tread when she
was sure her father could not possibly have found his way

back to the Beast's castle unaided through this trackless gloom. She shuddered at the thought of what her future held, her resolve to save her father from his terrible fate weakening. Then, without warning, the tree line simply ceased, and the snow faded away to be replaced by hock high brown and emerald ferns and grasses blooming under a warm sun. Before them ran an old wall thick with moss and ivy, its top higher than a tall man standing on a saddle could reach. It was as though in a morning they had ridden from winter into spring. Here indeed was enchantment.

The scene is told from Beauty's point of view, and is a series of images, principally father and daughter moving from the dark, snow-bound forest (which in part could also symbolize the despair that is gripping their lives) into the enchanted, permanently springlike weather enveloping the Beast's castle (a contrasting symbol of the start of a new phase in their lives). More important than this symbolism, however, the description gives the reader a sense of place *while at the same time* foreshadowing the magic in the story. This is very important because it prepares both Beauty and the reader for future magical events that may happen. We also have information about how Beauty is understandably nervous about the unknown future for which she has volunteered, and how morose and guilt-ridden her father seems.

If this same passage is written as a bridging section between two scenes, however, we may suppose a great deal—though perhaps not all—of the above information has already been conveyed to the reader. As a result, we can make the passage much shorter and less cinematic. All we are really trying to accomplish in the example below is get the characters from Scene A, Beauty's decision to go to the Beast's castle with her father, to Scene B, the first time Beauty and the Beast meet. We might be able simply to write, *The next day Beauty and her father arrived at the enchanted castle.* Although there's not much grace in the sentence, and it's pretty bald, under certain circumstances it would work fine. However, I'm assuming that there is still some information to give the reader.

In the following example we are "telling" a great deal more than we "showed" in the last example, but the information is going to set up some of the motivation (her fears) for Beauty's negative reaction to the Beast at their first meeting. We are also setting up the fact, as before, that the Beast lives in an enchanted castle. Indeed, we actually state that fact ("Here, it seemed, was proof that the Beast's castle was in the grip of powerful magic."). It is better to use a bridging passage like this as the point at which to convey to the reader that Beauty is "preoccupied," that is, worried—if not fearful—of her future, than to have to explain later why she reacts as she does to the Beast, which then serves as an editorial comment and weakens the dramatic action.

## 7.1.2   Indirect Narrative

Beauty rode in silence by her father's side, through the cold, intimidating dark woods, her thoughts preoccupied with what her future held. By the time they cleared the tree line and reached a high, ivy-covered brick wall she scarcely noticed how the dense winter bleakness of the forest had given way to springlike weather, quite out of keeping with the season. Here, it seemed, was proof that the Beast's castle was in the grip of powerful magic.

## 7.2   *Flashbacks and Flashforwards*

Flashbacks are more difficult to use than they at first appear to be, and can be misused. Poor use of flashback often suggests that you haven't really come up with the best way to dramatize the impact of a backstory on the present. Try to avoid flashbacks if possible.

The flashback should have a distinct purpose, revealing the backstory that runs parallel with, and clarifies the action in the main story. In Oscar Hijuelos's 1990 Pulitzer Prize–winning novel, *The Mambo Kings Play Songs of Love*, the main thrust of the novel's narrative is set up as a flashback by the opening paragraph:

> It was a Saturday afternoon on La Salle Street, years and years ago when I was a little kid, and around three o'clock Mrs. Shannon, the heavy Irish woman in her perpetually soup-stained dress, opened her back window and shouted out into the courtyard, "Hey, Cesar, yoo-hoo, I think you're on television, I swear it's you!" When I heard the opening strains of the "I Love Lucy" show I got excited because I knew she was referring to an item of eternity, that episode in which my dead father and my Uncle Cesar had appeared, playing Ricky Ricardo's singing cousins fresh off the farm in Oriente Province, Cuba, and north in New York for an engagement at Ricky's nightclub, the Tropicana.
>
> This was close enough to the truth about their real lives . . .

This is a fairly typical way to segue into a flashback. There is the sense, first of remembering ("It was a Saturday afternoon . . . years and years ago . . . "), then of subtly shifting to a more immediate present ("When I heard the opening strains of the 'I Love Lucy' show I got excited . . ."), then the "teasing" flashes of hindsight recollection that will become important as the narrative develops (". . . that episode in which my *dead* father . . . ." and "This was *close enough* to the truth"). The use of tenses is very important in the flashback, and it is one of the reasons they are deceptively difficult to write well. If you're not careful, you can tie yourself and your readers in knots figuring out past, present, and future in the narrative.

Another common problem with flashbacks is figuring out how to get back to the present. The solution is largely tied to the sort of story framework you have created around the flashback. Sometimes a simple white-space break is the best way. The episode in the past finishes, we pause a moment, and the present time story continues.

A good test of whether or not to use a flashback is to ask yourself, Does the story's progression of scenes (including flashbacks) seem natural?

If the answer is yes, then the flashback is valid. If not, it should be reconsidered and the story kept in the present. Note how Muriel Spark uses flashback and flashforward in *The Prime of Miss Jean Brodie*. By rights, the reader should be completely bewildered by all the shifting in time this short passage covers.

Rose Stanley believed [Monica], but this was because she was indifferent. She was the least of all the Brodie set to be excited by Miss Brodie's love affairs, or by anyone else's sex. And it was always to be the same. Later, when she was famous for sex, her magnificently appealing qualities lay in the fact that she had no curiosity about sex at all, she never reflected upon it. As Miss Brodie was to say, she had instinct.

"Rose is the only one who believes me," said Monica Douglas.

When she visited Sandy at the nunnery in the late nineteen-fifties, Monica said, "I really did see Teddy Lloyd kiss Miss Brodie in the art room one day."

"I know you did," said Sandy.

She knew it even before Miss Brodie had told her so one day before the end of the war, when they sat in the Braid Hills Hotel eating sandwiches and drinking tea which Miss Brodie's rations at home would not run to.

*The Prime of Miss Jean Brodie* is a tour-de-force in the liquid way it shifts time. Miss Brodie is a charismatic teacher at a Scottish girl's school between World War I and World War II, and the story is about her and the girls who fall under her spell. The novel is told mainly from Sandy's point of view, beginning in the 1930s when the girls are seniors, and moving backward in time to the late 1920s when they were juniors and most under Miss Brodie's spell, though it frequently jumps forward in time to the 1950s to see what has happened to the girls as adults.

The reason the novel works as well as it does is because it has the implicit tone of a narrator who can indulge, as we all do sometimes when telling stories aloud, in going backward and forward from the main event—the ultimate betrayal of Miss Brodie. Sandy invents a story and contrives Miss Brodie's dismissal from her teaching post and seat of power as revenge for Miss Brodie's having convinced one of Sandy's friends to go off and fight the fascists in the Spanish Civil War, where she is killed. The book, in part, seems almost a confession by Sandy for the guilt she still feels over her act of revenge.

Kurt Vonnegut's *Slaughterhouse Five* is another masterpiece of time-shifting narrative, as is John le Carré's *A Perfect Spy*. Martin Amis's *Time's Arrow* narrates the life of a Nazi war criminal by moving backward, beginning with his death and concluding with his birth. The results are disturbing for the reader as the story approaches and deals with the horrors of the Holocaust.

## 7.3 Transitions of Time–2

Transitions of chronological time are easier. A commonly used and accepted transitional technique is simply to leave a white space between one scene and the next, which is the equivalent of a jump cut in a movie. However, a reader still sometimes needs to be told how much time has passed between Scene A and Scene B. For example, *"Two days later, George again found himself in his boss's office,"* or, *"It had been ten years since . . ."*

When you create a story through a series of linked scenes, this white-space technique can be an effective way to define the beginning and end of a scene, regardless of chapter structure. It allows you a variety of structural options that do not necessarily tie you down to a chapter-by-chapter form of storytelling. My novel *Werewolf*, for example, is structured in terms of events that take place over about two weeks. Each chapter is quite long and is named for a day of the week. Yet the scenes within the day-by-day framework are deliberately quite short. Among other things, this allows the reader a chance to take a break from the text, if they wish to, and seems visually far less daunting.

Strange as it may seem, books written in small sections like this actually encourage readers to keep turning the page. The average reader hates to put a book down in the middle of a chapter or block of text because they worry they will lose the context, so they often won't begin what appears to be a long, daunting passage of prose. When confronted with smaller sections, however, readers say to themselves, "I'll just read these next few pages," each time they reach the end of a section. Before they know it, they're still reading long after they decided not to. The white-space technique in *Werewolf* lets readers move between the parallel action of the two main characters' viewpoints without disorienting them, and also allows for flashbacks where they are needed.

Sometimes, scenes that could be separated by a white space could be linked by a simple, brief, bridging passage so that the narrative prose flows better. For example, in Scene One, John has an argument with his wife, ostensibly over smashing up the car. In Scene Two, John goes to his girlfriend for solace. The bridging passage is probably a paragraph as simple as:

John slammed the front door and marched the ten blocks to the bus stop. Thirty minutes later the bus dropped him off two blocks from Sally's house.

The experience of the journey, as Zen masters tell us, is at least as important as arriving at the destination. The deftness with which we construct the *journey* through foreshadowing, establishing motivation, and careful revelation of important detail, to reach that *destination*—the story's denouement—takes real skill. When we reread a well written story for a second or third time, knowing where we are going allows us to appreciate that journey even more and makes the reading experience richer.

## 7.4   Exercises

- Making margin notes as you go, reread a story synopsis you've developed and figure out the important scenes to be dramatized. After that, decide whether they should be in direct or indirect narrative. Where could you use summaries without undermining the building drama of the piece?

- Go over a short story you have written, make a brief synopsis of the main points of the story line, and rewrite the whole story as indirect narrative. Then redramatize each plot point as a dramatic scene. Compare the two versions and see if you can combine them into one story without repeating anything. If the new version is shorter than the original, it is probably more effective. On the other hand, if the original version of the story is now expanded because you initially used too much indirect narrative, that's okay, too.

# 8

# Style: Saying It with Grace

"If you can say a thing with one stroke, unanswerably you have style."

*—George Bernard Shaw*

Discussing style is somewhat akin to discussing love or good taste; it is different things to different people. The best a writing teacher can do is offer mechanical advice ("Do this, don't do that") and recommend examples for students to study.

As a general rule, editors and agents are more likely to help an author develop a weak story if it's well written because it's much easier to fix flawed plotting than it is to teach graceful writing. So what can a writer do to acquire good style?

## 8.1  Write in a Style the Story Demands

The best way to acquire good style is to read and study the work of writers who are stylistically graceful. What I mean by grace is language that elicits spontaneous admiration. The point is *not* to emulate them, but to try and understand what makes their writing elegant.

Here, for example, is how Robert Goddard in *In Pale Battalions* describes a woman's recollection of her well-to-do world in England as a young girl:

> The first time I heard about Thiepval was a day I shall never forget. It was a Saturday in August 1932, a day of humid, oppressive warmth, thunder threatening but never arriving, a clammy air of menace thickening round Meongate as the day lengthened. Olivia was to give a party that evening. Previously a rarity, there had been several such events that summer, the guest of honour and Olivia's principal dancing partner on each occasion being Sidney Payne, the wealthy Portsmouth builder.
>
> I was fifteen then, possessed of sufficient false airs and fragile graces to take a scornful view of this sudden introduction of raucous gaiety.

When we read this passage, we feel Goddard has captured both the truth of this oppressive late summer day and the nature of the naïve young girl in prose that is rhythmically pleasing and concise. Nothing has been left to chance. Technique is subservient to the artist's vision, which we instinctively recognize is honest.

In Chapter 5 I mentioned the two 1993 sequels to Jane Austen's *Pride and Prejudice* (published in 1813). Following is an example from one of them. Julia Barrett is the pen name of professional writers Julia Braun Kessler and Gabrielle Donelly. This is how they begin *Presumption*, which is clearly not written by Jane Austen, though from the excerpt alone you might be forgiven for thinking so:

> If, as the prevailing wisdom has had it these many years, a young man in possession of a good fortune is always in want of a wife, then surely the reverse must prove true as well: any well-favored lady of means must incline, indeed yearn, to improve her situation seeking a husband.

Yet our own heroine found herself in the singular position of contesting this complacent assurance. Miss Georgiana Darcy, of Pemberley in Derbyshire, although beautiful, accomplished and, moreover, an heiress to a considerable fortune, remained nevertheless, at the age of seventeen years, markedly disinclined to secure her future happiness by bestowing that fortune upon any one. Georgiana had reason.

It is the deliberate style of the narrative, and the choice of such language ("a young man in possession of a good fortune," "in the singular position," "markedly disinclined," etc.) and long, complex sentences that give the *impression* of Regency prose. In fact, Jane Austen's prose was as sharp as her wit, and her sentences direct and not nearly so complex. However, this is a good example of trying to fit the style to the subject matter.

W. Somerset Maugham, a master of style, said, "I like a story that fits . . . . The storyteller . . . follows a design in his mind, leaving out this and changing that; he distorts facts to his advantage, according to his plan; and when he attains his object produces a work of art." Here's a passage from Maugham's short story "Mr. Know-All." The narrator has discovered he will share his cabin on an oceangoing liner with an English-speaking Levantine who quickly earns the dislike of his fellow passengers by knowing too much and announcing his knowledge too often. The artful simplicity of Maugham's resonant prose is exceptionally difficult to achieve and worth noting:

When I went on board I found Mr. Kelada's luggage already below. I did not like the look of it; there were too many labels on the suitcases, and the wardrobe trunk was too big. He had unpacked his toilet things, and I observed that he was a patron of the excellent Monsieur Coty; for I saw on the washing-stand his scent, his hairwash and his brilliantine. Mr. Kelada's brushes, ebony with his monogram in gold, would have been all the better for a scrub.

I did not at all like Mr. Kelada. I made my way into the smoking-room. I called for a pack of cards and began to play patience. I had scarcely started before a man came up to me and asked me if he was right in thinking my name was so and so.

"I am Mr. Kelada," he added, with a smile that showed a row of flashing teeth, and sat down.

True style is shaped by the honesty of a writer's vision, and it is reflected in every line of prose he writes. It is about choices: the words you choose, the way you use them, the music of your language, and the topics you choose to write about. Fay Weldon's style is well suited to her acerbic wit. The following is from *The Lives and Loves of a She Devil*, her wickedly funny novel about how Ruth gets her revenge on her husband, Bobbo, who leaves Ruth and the children for Mary Fisher, a successful writer of romance novels:

Mary Fisher finished a novel, *The Far Bridge of Desire*, and submitted it to her publisher; it was returned for extensive alterations. She was alarmed, upset and disconcerted. For if Mary Fisher had lost her touch, if a million million women stirred in their Valium dreams, reached for a Mary Fisher novel and sank back into slumber again, disappointed, that was tragedy indeed . . . .

And why had it happened? She couldn't understand it. She had taken more care with this novel than with many another . . . . She'd shown it to Bobbo during its writing, as any loving woman would her man, and he had even helped her with it.

Such narrative style would not work nearly as well when dealing with the more serious subjects tackled by such writers as Louise Erdrich or Ruth Rendel. Style involves the way you punctuate, how you vary the length of your sentences, their music and rhythm, how you break your text into paragraphs.

Charles Dickens, for example, even with his more serious novels such as *Hard Times*, has the air of the gossip about him that belies the sophistication of his style, even in this descriptive passage.

A sunny midsummer day. There was such a thing sometimes, even in Coketown.

Seen from a distance in such weather, Coketown lay shrouded in a haze of its own, which appeared impervious to the sun's rays. You only knew the town was there, because you knew there could have been no such sulky blotch upon the prospect without a town. A blur of soot and smoke, now confusedly tending this way, now that way, now aspiring to the vault of Heaven, now murkily creeping along the earth, as the wind rose and fell, or changed its quarter: a dense formless jumble, with sheets of cross light in it, that showed nothing but masses of darkness—Coketown in the distance was suggestive of itself, though not a brick of it could be seen.

And this is how Charles Palliser emulates Dickens's style in his 1989 prize-winning novel, *The Quincunx*:

Our house, the garden, the village, and the country for a mile or two thereabouts—this was my world, for it was all I had known, until that last summer when a new one opened before me at Hougham. And now that I seek an image for the undertaking I am embarked upon, I recall a glorious afternoon during that summer when— still unaware that I was to leave so soon—I escaped from the confinement under which I had long chafed and lay, exulting not so much in my freedom as in my having stolen it, on the bank of the stream that ran through

Mortseywood and on to the forbidden land towards the North.

Ernest Hemingway's style, by contrast, is one of contrived simplicity, though it contains unexpected traces of the exotic. He was one of the most influential stylists of the twentieth century, and, when his first novel *The Sun Also Rises* was published in 1926, its blunt language almost cost Max Perkins, Hemingway's editor at Scribner's, his job. Hemingway's direct, choppy prose changed forever the lingering Victorian style of an overt narrator that had been falling out of fashion. His writing style explored the newfound freedoms of expression, particularly in fashion, art, and manners that took place after World War I. He wrote in the simple, direct language of the working man, and his style shows his determination to reach those who profess a suspicion of intellectuals and would rather watch a ball game than read a book. This is how he begins *The Old Man and the Sea*:

> He was an old man who fished alone in a skiff in the Gulf Stream and he had gone eighty-four days now without taking a fish. In the first forty days a boy had been with him. But after forty days without a fish the boy's parents had told him that the old man was now definitely and finally *salao*, which is the worst form of unlucky, and the boy had gone at their orders in another boat which caught three good fish the first week.

## 8.2    Consider the Literal Meaning of Your Prose

Concerned with being "subtle" and "evocative," writers often forget that what they write must first make literal sense. Clumsy writers, for example, will say "he moved his hand," rather than, "he moved *a* hand," forgetting that he has *two* hands. This is not pedantry, but a precise use of language to say what you mean *exactly*.

Most writers of fiction like to think they are striving for poetic beauty in their prose without really knowing what that means. Poor or clumsy language is the bane of the novice writer. Here's an example of what I mean: *"Impatience darkened the gold of her hazel eyes."* First of all, how can impatience darken anything? It is inanimate. Secondly, how can hazel eyes be gold at the same time? The phrase *sounds* sort of poetic, but makes no sense. Here's another example: *"Sunlight pelted the window, dappling the furniture."* Sunlight can't pelt anything. What exactly does "bone weary" really mean? We see it in novels all the time, and, though we all *think* we know what it means, it rarely makes any kind of sense. Beware words or phrases that seduce with their sound without actually meaning anything. Good poetry, even when the writer is experimenting with the language, *always* makes sense if you study it long enough. Poetic prose should do no less.

Every writer should read, reread, and then put into practice the suggestions in Strunk and White's *The Elements of Style*. It is probably the best book ever written on the subject.

## 8.3   Say It with One Stroke

Style is about *seeing* something and then, in a pithy turn of phrase, "one stroke" as Shaw puts it, capturing its essence. A strong writing style is *not* about a superficial facility with words, but a writer's ability to observe truths about the world and express them evocatively. In this sense, writers of prose and writers of poetry share a common purpose in their efforts to use the English language at its most accurate and potent.

How, then, should we react to the following excerpt? I have deliberately delayed identifying it.

"Shall I clean your boots? Look, I'll get down and lick them." And, my brothers, believe it or kiss my sharries, I got down on my knees and pushed my red yahzick out a mile and half to lick his grahzny vonny boots. But all this veck did was kick me not too hard on the rot. So then it seemed to me that it would not bring on the sickness and pain if I just gripped his ankles with my rookers tight round them and brought this grahzny bratchny down on the floor. So I did this and got a real bolshy surprise, coming down crack amid loud laughter from the vonny audience. But viddying him on the floor I could feel the whole horrible feeling coming over me, so I gave him my rooker to lift him up skorry and up he came. Then just as he was going to give me a real nasty and earnest tolchock on the litso Dr Brodsky said:

"All right, that will do very well." Then this horrible veck sort of bowed and danced off like an actor while the lights came up on me blinking and with my rot square for howling. Dr Brodsky said to the audience: "Our subject is, you see, impelled towards the good by, paradoxically, being impelled towards evil . . . .

Out of context, a reader might consider this the work of an overindulgent writer. Why invent these weird words and make the narrative so difficult to follow?

The excerpt is from Anthony Burgess's *A Clockwork Orange.* The novel deals with the alienation of brutal adolescents from society and how one, Alex, is used as a subject for a scientific experiment to "bring him back to the fold." It's chilling to consider that the novel was first published in 1962, and yet seems more appropriate to today's world of alienated teenagers shooting and stabbing each other over sneakers and Starter jackets than do the battles of teenage gangs called Mods and Rockers in England that inspired the novel.

The novel questions whether Alex's brutal behavior is any worse than the deliberate crushing of his personality and will by the state. Because the novel is told from Alex's point of view, it is the style of the novel, the language that Alex uses to narrate his story, as much as the brutal crimes he commits, that set him apart. The invented language is deliberately designed to heighten this alienation. Burgess actually teaches us the slang he's invented as we read through the novel, so following the story is not as difficult as it first appears. The language also has the added function of taking the sting out of what might otherwise be very exploitive descriptions of Alex's vicious crimes of sex and violence, allowing us the safety of an arm's-length emotional distance from what we're reading.

What is the difference between *A Clockwork Orange* and this example? "*Mirrorflashes from highabove stained glass windows, pattering like colored TV snow on the oakpanelled lectern, he throatcleared and fronted to the birdchirping congregation, all atither, gripping the wooden rails with knucklewhite fists . . .* "

Though exaggerated, it is clearly intrusive storytelling and ego-driven word juggling masquerading as the kind of style the writer thinks an Anthony Burgess or Dylan Thomas might use. First of all, the passage is written in the third person, not first person, so the need to invent words is not nearly so compelling. Second, the invention itself is poor. "See how brilliant I am," the writer is proclaiming. "Applaud my dexterity with words, my linguistic inventiveness, my pyrotechnical skills. Look at *me*, never mind the story. What a stylist I am." Such prose is, at its heart, the work of an insecure and extroverted writer who is using linguistic gymnastics and the hollow sounds of words that have no real meaning to cover up inadequate storytelling skills.

Such a writer makes a basic assumption that is flawed, which is that writing takes second place to some sort of literary fashion. This is simply not true, though there are obvious stylistic differences marking the prose of a late-twentieth-century writer from that of his Victorian counterpart and the eighteenth-century novelist. Jane Austin, Charles Dickens, Virginia Woolf, Ernest Hemingway, E. L. Doctorow, and Tama Janowitz are clearly in a stylistically evolving line that reflects the tastes of their reading public as much as anything.

## 8.4   Words as Tools

Shape your sentences to do your bidding. They are powerful tools with which to carve out your story. One of the best ways to fix clumsy prose is to read it aloud. It will help you to catch monotonous, repetitious, and generally weak language, and it will expose the ungainly music of your words. Too many sentences with similar construction will bore the reader. Avoid the present tense in favor of the past tense, which is more commonly used in narrative style. Use an active voice rather than a passive one. Many beginning writers mistake the notion of passive voice for the tale form of narrative ("Let me tell a story about . . ."). The difference is (passive), "I *was bitten* by your dog," and (active), "Your dog *bit* me."

Don't try to write to please others, for you will never succeed. The suggestions of an editor or agent are only valid if they make sense to a writer who can suspend his ego and subjectivity long enough to analyze objectively the accuracy and usefulness of the comments. Nine times out of ten, the suggested changes will echo what you already knew about your story's weaknesses but were unsure or undecided about making until your inner suspicions were confirmed aloud by others.

Adjectives and adverbs are literary spices and, like all spices, should be used sparingly. As a rule of thumb, use only strong nouns and verbs in your writing, and let them carry their own weight unaided and without qualification. It is not a "tall building," for example, but "a skyscraper." Go on an adjective and adverb hunt—and kill them mercilessly.

Adjectives are said by some to be the enemy of nouns, and their misuse weakens the very nouns the writer wants to bolster.

In *The Elements of Style*, William Strunk calls misused qualifiers "leeches that infest the pond of prose, sucking the blood
of words." He added, "The adjective hasn't been built that can
pull a weak or inaccurate noun out of a tight place."

The adverb, on the other hand, is the enemy of the verb. It
is not meant to change a verb, but to create friction with it or
modify its meaning. Any adverb that ends in "-ly" may well be
an adjective in disguise, propping up a weak verb. "Richard
*angrily hit* Christopher" is better said, "Richard *slapped* Christopher." A good rule of thumb is that you are strengthening
your prose if you reduce the number of words needed to convey what you want to say. "Jane *removed her clothes* slowly" would
be better said, "Jane *undressed* slowly."

Somerset Maugham was so against such qualifiers that he
deliberately wrote an entire book (his autobiography, *Summing
Up*) without using a single adjective. This is how he uses
qualifiers in a short story called "The Verger":

> "A very nice christening, I thought, sir. Funny 'ow the
> baby stopped cryin' the moment you took him."
>
> "I've noticed they very often do," said the vicar, with a
> little smile. "After all, I've had a good deal of practice
> with them."
>
> It was a source of subdued pride to him that he could
> nearly always quiet a whimpering infant by the manner in
> which he held it and he was not unconscious of the amused
> admiration with which mothers and nurses watched him
> settle the baby in the crook of his surpliced arm. The
> verger knew that it pleased him to be complimented on
> his talent.

Maugham's use of qualifiers is subtly powerful. He deliberately modifies the picture of a "smile" on the vicar's face by
making it "little." This gives us a clearer picture of the vicar,
whose patronizing attitude is disguised as humility. Similarly,
Maugham underlines this portrait by mentioning the vicar has

a "subdued pride" that is fed by the "amused admiration" of the mothers and nurses of which he is "not unconscious." This last is a particularly interesting choice of words because the pedant, or the hapless editor who lacks an ear for irony or the music of language, would rewrite that as simply "he was *conscious*." The negative form, however, is clearly deliberate and in keeping with Maugham's subtle portrait of false humility in the vicar.

## 8.5   Imagery

The writer needs to consider carefully the purpose of imagery. It should create a mood or a clear, instant mental picture: *The sea, that warm Caribbean night, was like a burnished mirror. It reflected the light of the full moon like a silver road leading away from the ship.* We can use it to exaggerate: *The airplane's engine sounded like a cat had got caught in some empty tin cans.*

We use imagery to reach the reader's senses. The only way writers can really convey sight, sound, touch, or smell is to describe something universal enough that it evokes an instant image and so saves paragraphs of meaningless, long-winded prose. Your vision and appreciation of the world around you is what gives your imagery its potency. A car can "hurtle" down a hill, for example, but if you describe it as a "black missile," you are giving us a cliché and clumsy picture. Cars really can't move *that* fast, and the image creates confusion and makes the prose stumble.

Savor Ronald Hardy's description, in *The Wings of the Wind*, of a man examining a large, old leather Bible: "*He turned the pages and the spine cracked again with its sound of tiny cracking bones.*" What a terrific image that makes.

In the excerpt from Toni Morrison's *Jazz*, quoted in Chapter 4, we get this wonderful image: "*Opinions, decisions popped through the crowd like struck matches.*" It is then followed by a passage of machine-gun-like dialogue that wonderfully ampli-fies that image of opinions spreading like wildfire. Brilliant and evocative writing like this is what makes reading fiction such a uniquely rich experience.

Imagery helps us translate the abstract into the everyday: *John's depression was so intense he felt he was trapped in a dark, deep well.* In general, if you can't say it in *a very few, well chosen words,* odds are you probably shouldn't use it.

Rather than fix the clumsiness of their prose, some writers try to make virtues out of their faults. They claim that man-nerisms, bad grammar, clichés, repetition, and slang are all just "part of my style" and are therefore legitimate and accept-able regardless of whether or not the style is appropriate to the story. They're wrong. Poor writing is poor writing, and no amount of bluster or exhortations to respect individualism will change that fact.

Style is concerned with form, not content, and more often than not it will determine what gets read and what is rejected. In general, write simply and positively. Use active words that appeal to the senses—sight, sound, smell, and touch—putting your emphasis, if there is one, at the end of the sentence.

Style is about your individualism, honestly and gracefully expressed. The "rules" about writing and style are there to stop literary pratfalls, and if you have to break a few to be yourself in a story—and as long as you continue to hold a reader firmly—go ahead. Just know what rule you're breaking when you do it.

## 8.6   Exercise in Style

- Write a page of fiction using every cliché and poor writing technique you can think of. The point of this exercise is to make you conscious of when you write badly. Once you are aware of bad style, you'll find it easier to spot in your own work. For many reasons, most of them psychological, this is a particularly difficult exercise to do. You might want to repeat this exercise over a period of time, saving each version so that you can glance back at it and judge your writing then, using the objectivity of hindsight, against how you write now.

# 9

# Structure: Fitting It All Together

"Writing is manual labor of the mind: a job, like laying pipe."

—*John Gregory Dunne*

Structure is the glue that holds together the various elements of storytelling. Structure is concerned with *how* all the pieces fit together concisely and elegantly—the mechanics of it all.

Each story has a natural structure, and it is your difficult job to discover what that is. In other words, to find the most effective way to tell a particular story, you need to find the best frame to hold your story together. Sometimes you'll discover it early on, in the planning stage. At other times it won't happen until you're revising a first or even second draft of your story.

By figuring out the best structure for a story, you are really struggling to achieve an overview of your work. You need to be able to distinguish *what* the story is, from *how* you intend to tell it. They are *not* the same things. This is a fundamental element of good storytelling.

Without structure there is no real story because events and characters exist in a natural chaos on which the storyteller must impose order. At its most elemental, this order is: beginning, middle, and end—or, put another way: setup, confrontation, and resolution.

Understanding the structure of a novel inevitably leads a reader to the heart of the piece so that she can understand what she has read and what the writer was trying to do. Most often, the one thing editors have to straighten out before a book is published is weak structure.

Structure requires of a writer discipline and flexibility of mind, but, principally, it involves reading and rereading what you've written. You must know *where* you are going, *what* is becoming implicit in your story—the *why* of it all. You must become aware of the complexities you didn't intend to write but which are now present, the layers. You must have the courage to delete words and paragraphs and whole chapters by restructuring each sentence, and make sure you *show* (not tell) the reader what is important, by rearranging and tightening the pacing of information.

## 9.1 What the Story Is and How You Tell It Are Not the Same

Beyond dramatizing a story worked out in advance rather than developed in a rambling fashion, most writers are in the dark about exactly what they've written until the first draft is completed. Structure implies deliberate decisions about *how* a story is going to be told, and it is intimately bound up with a need to understand *what* it is you've written—a not-so-obvious statement.

What I mean by this is that all stories have implications. Unplanned events in a story cause ripples that should be taken into account. Attention to structure demands that the implications of events in a story are recognized and somehow accommodated. Failure to do so undermines a story's potential and perhaps consigns it to the rejection pile.

Here's an example of what I mean. We plot our story this way:

A repressed, nervous young woman living in a big city one day gets so frightened by something that she goes out and buys a gun. Soon after, she kills a man whom she believes was about to attack her. She then returns to her parents' home to await her trial on charges of manslaughter. The event has changed her personality, however. She is at last willing and able to stand up for herself, and as a result finds for the first time the freedom to redefine her relationship with her domineering father.

There are a number of ways to write this story. Here's one:

We begin with the young woman arriving back at her parents' home for the first time in many years, and, as the story develops, we concentrate on the power struggle between father and daughter. We gradually reveal what has happened in a series of scenes of character conflict. Seemingly ordinary events, such as going to the store, having a meal, watching the television, and so on, become suffused with new meaning as the full extent of what the daughter has done before she came home is revealed.

In our original synopsis of the story, we plan for the shooting incident to take place in a subway car. However, as we dramatize the scene, something unplanned happens: In the course of defending herself with her pistol, our heroine also wounds an innocent teenager who is hit by a stray bullet.

The emphasis of the story begins to shift. Instead of the story simply being about how standing up for yourself is an empowering decision, it is now potentially about how far we should go in standing up for ourselves, a more intricate moral dilemma.

There are now choices to make in the direction your story

should take: On the one hand, you can ignore this added complication of an innocent victim. The main thrust of the story can remain the young woman's struggle to define who she is by learning to stand up for herself. On the other hand, if you incorporate this unplanned element, its reverberations through the story will significantly alter or modify relationships and events you thought you had figured out.

Taking this wrinkle into account will mean substantially deviating from your original synopsis. It might be advisable to pause in the writing process and come up with a revised synopsis that will allow you to write a less contrived, more honest story. The deciding factors should be (a) whether you should trust your subconscious and write a story that is as true to life as possible, and (b) what you decide you want the theme of the story to be.

If you decide you don't want to utilize the wounding of the innocent bystander, you should probably rewrite the scene without that element.

Perhaps the maimed teenager has a brother who travels halfway across the country to confront his sister's assailant. His arrival at the young woman's house is the catalyst that finally releases the tension that has been building between father and daughter. The outcome is that they finally achieve some sort of peace, if not familial love, through this tragedy.

## 9.2 Structure and Point of View

Understanding structure will help you define the relationship between a *specific subject* or theme, a character, what happens to him or her, and why it happens. It will determine point of view and pacing of information.

The most obvious structural choice you can make in a story is its point of view, that is, who is telling the story. *How* a story is told is vital to its success or failure. It is easy for the unwary novelist to tell the reader too much or to tell it from the wrong perspective. If you're not careful, you won't just foreshadow what is going to happen in your story. You will tip off the reader to what the surprises are.

On the other hand, your storytelling may be so obtuse that readers lose interest because they can't figure out what's going on. A good example of how this delicate problem is successfully handled is Scott Turow's *Presumed Innocent*. Here, a first-person, apparently happily married narrator is forced to stand trial for the murder of his mistress, and the reader is left in doubt right until the end as to whether or not the narrator is guilty. This successful manipulation of suspense is what gives the book its page-turning quality. Did he or didn't he do it?

Poor structure is usually the reason a story is not working, even if the writer is talented. The parts seem to hang together, but both you and your readers are dissatisfied and neither knows exactly why, though readers will not hesitate to blame you for sloppy writing without being able to put their finger on exactly what it is that ruined the story for them.

Amy Tan's *The Joy Luck Club*, for example, is wonderfully written, but structurally the book is weak. The stories don't really link together or lead the reader anywhere. We are led to expect that the frame story, the modern-day story of the daughter taking her dead mother's place at a mah-jongg table, will lead us somewhere or, at the very least, come to a conclusion. Instead, the reader is left hanging, the story unfinished. While the chapters become short stories that comprise a sort of *Canterbury Tales* of immigrant Chinese mothers and their Chinese-American daughters, as a novel the story is unsatisfying because of this structural flaw. A much better example of how an author can use this approach is in Ray Bradbury's *The Illustrated Man*. The book is a collection of short stories within the framework of a man whose tattoos come to life, each with its own story to tell, with a frame story that introduces the book and wraps it up.

John le Carré's *The Russia House* is another novel with structural problems. Le Carré has a facility with language that most writers would give their right arms to possess. And yet, in a novel supposedly in the first person, we get to know the thoughts of another character in an entirely distracting and illogical manner. How can a reader accept that a first-person narrator knows the thoughts of another *as they think them* if he has to wait until the end of the novel to learn that "this is what so-and-so told me"? It destroys the novel's sense of unity, the fictional world it has created, and the coherence of the narrative. It betrays the pact with a reader that the author has set up. There is also a character in the first fifty pages with whom we spend a great deal of time but who does little more than set up the story then disappear, an example of poor pacing of information. Readers are led to believe this character will amount to something more because of the amount of time and emotional energy readers spend with him, only to be disappointed. Could we not have been told the important story information in this first fifty pages in a better way, more consistent with the story of the love affair that unfolds?

Chekhov once said, "If you pull a gun in Act I, you must fire it in Act III." In effect, le Carré produces the gun, but never fires it.

## 9.3 "Get Out of That"

Stephen King's novel, Misery, is about an author held captive by a lunatic fan who forces the author to write a book bringing back to life a heroine he has killed off. Misery is also, subtly, about how to write a commercial thriller. As we watch the new Misery Chastain novel develop, King talks about the "get-out-of-that" school of writing. What he means by this is to put your hero, unconscious, in a car that is just about to go crashing over the cliff and end the chapter. This is similar to the cliff-hanging movie serials that were so popular from the 1930s to the 1950s. Your task is to come up with a credible way to get the hero out of a predicament—to, in effect, "get out of that."

If, for example, you have your heroine tied to a railway line with the train thundering toward her, and then "solve" the problem by saying in the next paragraph, "With one bound she was free," you have cheated the reader. The technical term for such a lapse in the story is *a logic hole*. By destroying the fictive dream with an illogical event or scene, you sabotage your story. (The classical term for this is *deus ex machina*, or "god from a machine," an unexpected, artificial character or device suddenly introduced to resolve a situation or untangle a plot.)

John le Carré's novel, *A Perfect Spy*, is wonderfully structured. It cleverly intertwines two unfolding stories that share the unity of being about the same character at different points in his life. One is the autobiography of a spy who may or may not be a double agent. The other is the search for the spy, who has gone missing, by the man who recruited him many years before. Both stories finally come together in a logical resolution that leaves the reader entirely satisfied.

I would strongly recommend reading the stories of Daphne du Maurier and those of British novelist Robert Goddard, who has been hailed as "the new Daphne du Maurier." Their wonderful narrative styles and mastery of structure and circular plotting are equaled by few other writers. Goddard has been dubbed by critics on both sides of the Atlantic "the prince of plotting," with good reason.

## 9.4  Literary Nuts and Bolts

A writer's sense of structure is akin to a painter's intuitive yet considered choice of shape and color, or a jazz musician's instinctive improvisational ability. Instinctive art is the end result of constant practice, until your mastery of the techniques of your craft become second nature. You need to be able to spot and adapt to the implications that develop when characters take on substance in unexpected ways, the circularity of plot strands, the meaning of the denouement, in terms of what may happen next because of what has gone before.

Structure is concerned with nuts and bolts, the individual words as tools that you're using to put flesh on the skeletal story synopsis you've developed. Each comma, colon, semicolon, em dash, and period is part of the structure of a sentence and should have a specific function.

Each word should carry its own weight; each sentence is a part of the structure of a paragraph. An awareness of structure, a constant retuning of your work until it's right, is developed by studying craft until you acquire the skill to see what is all but invisible to the untutored eye. Mastering techniques provides you with the tools to create stories that seem effortlessly crafted. Only you should know how much sweat and hard work has gone into creating them.

# PART TWO

## Notes on the Storytelling Process

# 10

# On Getting Published

"A professional writer is an amateur who didn't quit."
                                        –*Richard Bach*

Let's start with a story:

On their twelfth birthday, twin brothers, one an optimist and the other a pessimist, were both asked to wait in separate stables filled with straw and left alone.

An hour later their parents looked in on the pessimist. He appeared most dejected and kept moaning, "What am I going to do with a room full of straw? This is the worst birthday present of my life."

However, when the parents looked in on the stable with the optimist they could barely make him out for the blizzard of flying straw that filled the air, and they could hear him muttering determinedly, "With all this straw there's just got to be a horse here somewhere."

You might want to bear this story in mind as you think about the things I've discussed in this book.

## 10.1    The Marketplace

For the less well known or first-time novelist, getting published can be a fantastically frustrating business. The publishing marketplace has become more demanding of novelists, especially first-time novelists, than ever before. There is much talk of the demise of the midlist book. These days, midlist books tend to be published novelists' option novels. Publishing houses are looking for "blockbusters" and "breakout" books, those novels that hit the best-seller lists and satisfy a seemingly insatiable corporate craving for ever larger profits, often at the expense of the inexperienced novelist. The genre market, which is where many first novelists used to get their start, goes in cycles. Often you hear of a "hot" genre, or one where there is a dearth of books, and by the time your novel is ready to be sent in it is too late. Don't watch the trends and deliberately try to ape a successful writer. Just try and write the very best you can. It is the uniqueness of *your* style, vision, and imagination that will eventually prove your strongest asset in getting published once they are fully developed. Outstanding fiction of any sort will always be in demand. It is the mundane though workmanlike piece of fiction that is tougher to publish these days.

What, paradoxically, works in an author's favor is that an editor's reasons for acquiring a book can be as idiosyncratic as those that led to writing it. One major reason for getting an agent is that the good ones know which editor is where and what his or her tastes are, which increases a novel's chances of publication. Another is that editors are also more inclined to take seriously an agented submission because the agent has already sorted some of the "wheat" from the "chaff." Editors anticipate that the reading experience will be more fruitful and enjoyable as a result.

Editors and agents are constantly surprised, frustrated, and overjoyed by what sells and what doesn't. We always think we know, but the truth is we rely mostly on instinct developed through years of reading, keeping an eye on what sells, and faith in our own educated taste. In the end, we can only pin our hopes on what inspires us.

## 10.2 The Acquiring Editor

It is neither the editor's nor the agent's job to teach novelists how to write, and yet at some point in a writer's career, especially early on, that's exactly what many editors and agents end up doing. More precisely, they help the writer go that last mile.

Publishing house editors need to show their colleagues nearly perfect manuscripts, and they don't have the time or energy (except in rare cases) to develop flawed but promising submissions. As a result, editorially skilled agents (many of whom, like me, were once publishing house editors) have emerged as the few remaining professionals in publishing able and willing to undertake this developmental work for free.

Editorial work should be invisible. It can be structural, helping the author distinguish *what* the story is, and then improving *how* it's told (a difference too many authors seem unaware of); or mechanical, cleaning up a phrase here or there, catching repetition, emphasizing a theme, pointing out a weakness in character development or a hole in the story's logic; but mostly the novels editors buy need to be all but ready for publication.

Once an editor finds something he or she likes, the editor then has to present it to an editorial board. In small houses, this can be limited to only a couple of other people, such as the subsidiary rights director, marketing director, and the publisher (who assess the book's commercial potential). In larger houses, the board can include many others, so don't take rejection personally. It's not about *you*, but the book, though I know it's often hard to make the distinction.

It's difficult for an editor to convince harried colleagues that, while a first novel may not be outstanding, the author is clearly talented and will come across with something wonderful on the second or third go-round. The argument usually goes, "Well let's see that one, then." The economics of publishing do not much allow for this type of nurturing, "old-fashioned" publishing any longer. A canny editor who falls in love with a book needs to convince colleagues (who may not have the editor's eye for talent) that the book has a dollars-and-cents potential if the book is to have any chance of getting published.

## 10.3   The Success or Failure of a Book

Paradoxically, in an industry designed to make money selling books, most published novels die on the vine because of little publicity or marketing support from the company. Reviewers are partially responsible for this situation. On the one hand, they complain about publishing company hype, but, by and large, they go along with the setup and pay attention only to "big" books while giving scant attention to other, sometimes more deserving, novels by lesser known writers who really could use the boost to their career that comes from good review publicity.

Reviews, advanced quotes, and publicity are important factors in the success or failure of a book. If a writer wishes to participate in launching his or her writing career, above and beyond the actual writing of a book, these are the most promising areas to work in, in cooperation with, ideally, a book publicist if you can afford one, and the publishing company's publicity department.

Many published writers harbor the misconception that, if only a publishing company would spend a lot of money on the promotion of their book, particularly in newspapers and magazines, the book would become a smash success. The truth is, when a book *is* advertised, the publisher is boasting not of the book's worth, but of its critical and numerical sales *success*. The difference is significant. The only time such advance media advertising is worthwhile is when the author happens to be a household name such as Stephen King, where the publicity is news about a new book, an event eagerly awaited by his many fans. A classic example of how publicizing a book's *success* helped generate momentum for its sales is Robert James Waller's novel *The Bridges of Madison County*. In 1993, *Bridges* went from comparative obscurity after it was first published by Warner Books, with virtually no promotional help from the publishing company when it first appeared in the book stores, to a stunning long life on the best-seller lists almost entirely because of a powerful, grass-roots, word-of-mouth campaign started by store owners and book buyers. This caught the publishing company completely off-guard and forced it to scramble to catch up with the growing popularity of the book. The moral is, no one knows why a best seller becomes so, and anyone who tells you differently is either a fool or a liar.

All this is not intended to put off would-be novelists, but to tell it as it is.

Tack this on the wall above your word processor:

If you are determined, and learn your craft, you will eventually get published.

Don't second-guess what's commercial—that's not your job, and editors and agents can tell a cynically written piece a mile off. All you can do is pour your heart and soul into the thing, submit it, and move on to the next piece, learning the lessons of craft as you go.

Remember:

The higher calling is not the Writer—
but the Storyteller.

## 10.4   First Steps in Getting Published

All this is intended to emphasize, underscore, and reiterate that a finished manuscript (at least in the writer's eyes) is the *only* form in which a story should be submitted, and almost certainly it is the only one that may eventually be bought. I get too many letters that accompany submitted manuscripts that say, "I know this needs work, but I don't know where or how to do it. Let me know what to do, and I'll be happy to make the changes that are needed."

If this describes you or your book, you've taken the right step in *learning* how to fix problems you know are present by studying a book like this on writing technique.

Don't expect an editor or agent to help you editorially. Chances are they won't. They don't need the extra work, and there are enough talented, *accomplished* storytellers ready for that first break. Make sure you're one of them when your turn comes.

If you're not put off by all of the above, then, like the optimist in the opening story, you've passed the first hurdle: In the face of absurd odds and difficulties, you have the obdurate determination and attitude it takes to stay the course. If you learn what needs to be learned, the odds are you'll be published eventually.

There's a story that bears telling here:

A young musician desired more than anything to study with a particular master violinist. One day, the pupil got his chance to play for the maestro. He arrived for the audition and played his heart out.

After he finished, there was a long silence. Then the maestro said, rather offhandedly, "Not enough fire," and with a wave of one hand dismissed the student. Now the student, as you can imagine, was devastated. In disgust he quit the violin and went into commerce, becoming a very successful businessman.

Many years later, when the maestro gave a recital at Carnegie Hall, the former student went backstage and introduced himself. He and the maestro had a pleasant discussion, but finally the student could not resist, and recounted their last meeting, when he had played for the old man and been told, "Not enough fire."

"What did you mean?" the student asked.

"Oh, I say that to everyone," the maestro said disarmingly.

The student was stunned, and then became very angry. "I could have been a great musician," he said. "Instead, because of *you*, I gave it up."

The maestro looked up, and with a smile said, "Not really. If you were going to be a great musician you'd have done it anyway, regardless of anything I said."

# 11

# On Writing Fiction

"In a mood of hope and faith my work goes on. A ream of fresh paper lies on my desk waiting for the next book. I am a writer and I take up my pen to write."

*–Pearl S. Buck*

Writing is not putting down words on paper—that's just hard labor. Writing is *editing*, or shaping, those words into scenes and images and layers and symbols, making sure each word, be it an "and" or a "but," carries its own weight. Learning to write a good novel, especially a hardcover-quality novel, is *very difficult.* Of the 250 million people in the United States, maybe sixty or so make a good living from writing fiction. You figure the odds.

So, don't expect to make a living writing fiction, at least for the early part of your career. Most novelists have to work at something else, too. But that means you are free to take as long as you need on a project, and you won't have to write to a deadline that will force you to compromise the quality of your work.

Talk to experienced, published writers, and you'll discover they all learned to write fiction basically the same way: They read a lot, and then wrote a lot of fiction, some of it excruciatingly bad, gradually improving as they figured out what they were doing wrong. If they were lucky, they got some helpful pointers from established writers or editors along the way.

## 11.1   The Perils of Factory Fiction

Some guides into unknown territory are better than others, and some guides have more sympathy than others for the tribulations of a neophyte venturing into the unknown. In the end, however, the quality of a writer's work is a reflection of an individual's philosophies about craft, study, and creativity.

Some well-known writers are disdainful of anyone's being able to teach creative writing in a meaningful way. They fear that what is being taught is mechanical "factory fiction" rather than worthwhile art that reflects the human condition in an entertaining way. In my view, this is a disingenuous attitude from these disdainful writers; books or classes in creative writing can only point the way. There is no magic formula, and the ambitious but uninspired writer who searches for it will never succeed. Studying writing through analysis or, more accurately, diagnosis, is not a justification for encouraging or perpetuating mediocrity.

## 11.2   Learn from the Best

Great storytelling skills, that is, powerful dramatization, elegant style, and good story sense are almost impossible to teach. One can teach only the opposite, that is, what a student shouldn't do, and hope that by inference and an eventual mastery of technique, the student will learn what should be done. A teacher can also expose the student to the best examples of storytelling and, by pointing out why, in the teacher's opinion, these are the best examples, hope that continued exposure to quality material will eventually have a positive effect. What you read will determine the kind of writer you become.

Because a writer is on the best-seller lists doesn't necessarily mean that, in terms of craft, his or her work is worth emulating. What is unique and marketable about an established writer who successfully breaks all the rules will not work for a carbon-copy writer trying to duplicate this success. Writers can't count on the blessings of fate—they can only hope for them. This is not a book about "making it" or becoming successful in the marketplace, for no one has any control over such things. The only sure path to publishing success is to master the craft of fiction and produce work that has merit and depth.

## 11.3   Guidelines for Successful Fiction

There are rules to writing fiction—at least, when you start. These rules are really only guidelines, of course, but they warn writers about the kinds of poor craftsmanship that can get them into trouble. Fiction writers need to learn what makes strong characterization, and why plotting ahead of time is so important. They need to understand the difference between suspenseful writing and coy and obtuse writing that will just irritate readers. Following the tenets of this book on basics and working with good writing teachers will give you an insight into what you should do, but in the end it is your determination to understand and intellect to perceive that will help you become a successful—and published—storyteller.

Pablo Casals, the world-famous cellist, once badly injured a hand in a mountain-climbing expedition and, when told he might never play again, said, "Thank God. At last I'm free." Two years later, he was again giving concerts and playing better than ever. Creative expression is an addiction beyond the creator's control, except in terms of how well we learn our craft. Writers write because they have to, not because they want to.

## 11.4 What Should I Write?

The question facing the tyro writer then, is, What should I write?

Although stories don't simply entertain, they should do that first and foremost. They reflect and interpret the world around us and make us aware of hypocrisy and paradox. They stir up emotions, and bring structure, order, and art to everyday chaos and randomness. A good story creates enlightenment out of pain and bewilderment.

Storytelling is very possibly the earliest art form prehistoric man practiced. Adventures of the hunt, deeds of bravery, incidents that thrilled and stirred an audience, stories that grandmothers told granddaughters, that shamans and priestesses told their acolytes—all passed along vital information that contributed to a clan's survival and growth. With each generation, the information developed and became more formal until, at a time when writing was still nonexistent or rudimentary, stories codified knowledge and set acceptable standards of behavior.

One reason the Don Juan tales of Carlos Casteneda have remained so popular since they first appeared in the early 1970s is that they are faint echoes of this oral tradition that resonate in our cultural consciousness. Here, the author straddles fact and fiction, making himself a character in his tales about a Mexican Indian shaman, Don Juan, who is passing along centuries-old knowledge through a series of offbeat lessons for the author. The real truths in these stories are not whether the incidents portrayed actually happened, but what the stories have to say about the human condition and our relationship to the world around us. Another example is Anne Rice's *Vampire Chronicles*, which features the oral history of the vampire mythology created by Rice. This oral storytelling tradition is also often a feature of a certain type of fiction by women authors, such as Laura Esquivel's *Like Water for Chocolate*, or Amy Tan's *The Joy Luck Club*.

Despite thousands of years of development and diversity of form, stories still perform essentially the same functions: They define our cultural identity, they deal with common fears and moral values, and they help us face up to and cope with death, loss, and other trauma.

## 11.5   Stories That Endure

Myths, legends, and fairy stories have endured because of their universality and have become the basis of many hundreds of stories. *David and Goliath* or *Cinderella* may today differ in relevance from the original intent of their authors, but they are profound enough to be invested with new meaning and thus continued validity for each generation that hears or reads them. Such stories are archetypes. *David and Goliath*, for example, which is about the lone underdog triumphing against overwhelming odds, clearly becomes the basis for a great deal of the mythology of the American western frontier. *Shane* by Jack Schaeffer or *Hombre* by Elmore Leonard are just two examples of many. Often, stories involving sports heroes are also in this vein.

Rossini composed an opera about Cinderella, Julie Andrews played her in a Rodgers and Hammerstein musical, Jerry

Lewis played a male version in a movie. By some counts, there are more than 2,000 versions of the story in a variety of differing cultures and languages, from Native American to Japanese. For some, the story is about a poor person making good and thus is relevant to the problems of minorities within society. For others, its theme of the need for a woman to marry in order to rise in society becomes a springboard to discuss contemporary women's issues. In many ways, *Oliver Twist* by Charles Dickens fits the Cinderella archetype. The same is true of *The Sound of Music*, Fielding's *Tom Jones* (a male Cinderella), and the myth of Pygmalion, which became, via a play by George Bernard Shaw, *My Fair Lady.*

Nearly all time-travel stories owe some debt to Washington Irving's "Rip van Winkle," from Nathaniel Hawthorne's "Wakefield" to Jack Finney's *Time and Again.*

Orpheus is an archetypal story of an epic descent into Hell that has formed the basis for Dante's *Inferno*, Bunyan's *Pilgrim's Progress*, Milton's *Paradise Lost*, Shakespeare's *King Lear*, Lewis Carroll's *Alice in Wonderland*, on up to Michael Crichton's best-selling *Jurassic Park.*

Certain tales wax and wane in popularity, reflecting the changing morals and ethics of generations. On one level, the best stories function as part of a collective societal dream, in which important current "information" (for example, about violence in the home or among the young, or the ethical dilemmas of abortion) is processed in creative and sometimes magical ways to enhance both our understanding of the problem and its possible solutions.

Charles Dickens makes his readers believe that the miser, Scrooge, in *A Christmas Carol* can, in one night, eschew bitterness and malevolence in favor of joy and compassion. In real life, such things don't happen, do they? But, through the strength of great storytelling, we can, for a moment, believe that they do, and in the flowering of such a belief we discover an optimism that the "bad" among us can indeed be reformed if only the right set of circumstances prevail.

## 11.6   The Good Storyteller

The good storyteller will show us that, beyond simple heroes and villains outwitting each other, the real story can be about one man's single-minded attempt to find meaning for himself and vindicate his beliefs. Yet, at the same time that he enriches human knowledge, he can also exact a terrible human suffering. The main character of such a story, who is left to ponder the awful price that he and others must pay because of his actions as he balances intent against results, is interesting and important to us. He is a more memorable creation than a character to whom we can simplistically ascribe blame or draw a fleeting sense of satisfaction for retribution delivered.

It is your job as a storyteller not to awaken readers from the fictional dream you are spinning while you tell your tale. This dream is more than a mundane suspension of disbelief. Like Alice falling through the looking glass, when we pick up a story and start to read, we quickly find ourselves in another world, populated by people who become our friends or guides to new experiences that amplify or explain the world around us. Like the children of Hamlin Town, we are enticed by characters who lead us we know not where, forgetful of all but the piper's music, seeing the real world suddenly afresh when the end is reached and the music finally fades to an echo. Beware a reader's wrath if you should rudely awaken him from this fictional dream world through clumsy technique or poor story-telling. The spell will be broken, and perhaps the reader will never again pick up one of your books.

Great stories, like great art, serve as a sort of societal conscience, and are about the trials and triumphs of the human spirit. Such stories are created by, among other things, honesty of vision, solid craft, and graceful prose.

One of the best descriptions of what makes a great short story was given by Stephen Vincent Benét (who wrote *The Devil and Daniel Webster*): "Something that can be read in an hour and remembered for a lifetime." With some modification for the time it takes to read the story, this definition applies equally to great novels.

# Appendix A

## A 15-Point Self-Editing Guide

Many a good story has been marred beyond the possibility of recovery by weak storytelling, and for first-time novelists in particular this can prove the difference between being published and being rejected. Some of the format suggestions that follow may seem arbitrary and overly conservative, but they all have a good reason for being (and that is to make an editor or agent's life easier and the reading experience as pleasant as possible). Ignore these suggestions at your peril.

Here, then, is a compact reminder of the main things you should be doing to your manuscript before you send it to either an agent or an editor, and why you should be doing it this way. Follow these points religiously, and you will almost certainly double your chances of getting published.

1. *Learn exactly what the requirements of a publishing house are before you submit something.* How? Call them. If a publishing house says, for example, no manuscripts under 80,000 words, and you submit a manuscript that's shorter than that, it will come straight back to you, probably unread. Don't send romances, however brilliant, to horror editors, or vice versa. If in doubt, a quick chat with the editorial assistant, if not the editor, will confirm whether or not to send the manuscript. If you wanted

a plumber, and a carpenter turned up instead, not only would the carpenter be useless, his appearance would aggravate the hell out of you.

2. *The look of a manuscript is the first thing an editor or agent sees. Put editors at ease from the start by making them anticipate the reading experience, not dread it.* Correct, professional presentation makes life a lot easier when you *have* to read dozens of submissions. If you were selling your car, or your home, you'd clean it and paint it, and present it in the best possible light. Treat your manuscript submission the same way. Who would you rather spend time with? Someone who is personable and presentable, or a self-absorbed, disheveled bum? Accordingly:

   a. *Double-space your manuscript.* No exceptions to this rule.

   b. *Don't use desktop publishing fonts, just regular typewriter courier or elite typefaces.* There is a reason for this. Most editors can judge word counts visually after a while, which helps them make early profit-and-loss estimates on the cost of a book, an important consideration in its publication. Strange fonts make life difficult and the reading experience a pain in the bum.

   c. *Use generous margins and keep the right-hand side ragged— no "justified" texts.* There is no such thing as truly "justified" text outside of professional typesetting, and manuscripts presented this way make the reading experience, once again, very aggravating. Margins are useful for jotting notes during the editorial process. Aim for about 200–250 words a page.

   d. *Paragraph frequently, but don't put a white space between each paragraph.* White spaces have a specific function in a manuscript, usually to do with a break in point of view or a passage of time. Indent each paragraph instead.

e. *Instead of using CAPITAL LETTERS to emphasize, underline.* It makes a typesetter's life (and thus also a proofreader's, which leads to a happy managing editor) much easier, as there are fewer chances of making *expensive* mistakes and major typesetting corrections during production. If you want to indicate italics, or computer type, or whatever, write "ital." or "computer face" next to the underlined words, and circle these words to ensure they are read as instructions.

f. *Always use a fresh ribbon or full toner cartridge.*

g. *Use continuous page numbering, with an author name and your title for the book along the top header on every page.*

h. *Leave the manuscript loose leaved, preferably in a box.*

i. *Use only one side of the paper, not both.*

j. *Make sure your name, address, and telephone number are on the title page.*

k. *Include a self-addressed, stamped envelope if you want the manuscript returned.*

l. *Check your grammar, and use your spell checker to check typos.* Read what you write carefully and often, even after using the spell checker. Check that your program hasn't okayed words that are spelled correctly but used improperly (such as "cam" instead of "came," or "their" instead of "there," for example). Study Strunk and White.

m. *Don't send your only copy. Don't send a worn-out version, either.* Editors, like dance partners, don't like to have it rubbed in that they were your last choice, even if they know it's probably true.

n. *Include a brief cover letter and a one-page synopsis of the story's beginning, middle, and end.* Don't treat editors or agents as you would regular readers. They're not, so don't "tease"—it's aggravating. Briefly tell them the whole story in the synopsis, because they want to see how you've structured your story. Don't get clever with the cover letter, because if you can't write a decent one-page cover letter, you sure as hell can't write a 300-page novel properly. Don't start, "Here's my first draft. If you like it I'll sit down and polish it"; or "I'm blind, deaf, and dumb, and just had my left leg amputated after an accident that occurred while I was standing in line waiting for my unemployment check. Here's my first novel, hope you like. I wrote it in the hospital," or variations thereof. Neither expect a response if your manuscript is returned. Only editors can handwrite messages to writers, if you're lucky enough to get one. You should *type* everything.

3. *Show, don't tell.* This common problem is a little more sophisticated than people think, because it is about judgment. You need to figure out what to show, and what to tell. Don't ever explain or get a character to do it for you. Find another way to present the information. The best rule of thumb is, try to describe as succinctly, objectively, and clearly as possible the "movie" that is running in your head, and whether a piece of plot information is important enough to merit its own scene. Note the difference between *"Damn it," he said angrily. Ruth took a step backward.* and, *"Damn it," he said, kicking over a chair. Ruth took a step backward.*

4. *Start each scene as closely as you can to the "meat" of the*

*action.* This will pace the book much better and make it read faster, with no loss of depth or subtlety. It will, however, force you to become more inventive and imaginative and not rely on "dead" prose.

5. *Be aware of the literal meaning of what you have written.* For example, "The spring sun pelted the window like marbles on glass." A nonsensical impossibility, for the sun can't pelt or have sound. Sleet, perhaps, but not the sun, or sunlight. "He picked up the newspaper and was soon absorbed in its pages." A rather nasty way to go. Or, "The policeman officiously snapped his bag shut. It all looked straightforward, clearly an open-and-shut case."

6. *Read what you have written aloud, but be aware that narrative, particularly third-person narrative, should sound different from speech.* Avoid "got," "nice," and "very" except in dialogue. Go on a "which" hunt and replace it with "that" wherever possible. Know the difference between "its" and "it's" and when to use them. Go on an adjective and adverb hunt. Kill them unmercifully. Strive for grace and clarity in your work. Read and reread *Strunk and White.*

7. *Be aware of the rhythm of your language, the length of your sentences, the musical ebb and flow of words and phrases, how one sentence sits in relationship to the next, and the one after that.*

8. *Avoid characters who whisper, roar, mumble, state, interject, fume, explode, or repeat each other's names endlessly.* "Said" is usually quite enough. It is an invisible word, and in some cases can be eliminated entirely.

9. *Keep your point of view consistent and as limited as possible.* Novels are about characters, not just plot. So don't swap points of view (POV) from one paragraph to another and, in general, from one character to another just to

explain the story. Pick a POV, start the story with it if you possibly can, and try to stick to it throughout the novel. That way we can empathize with one character and feel her fear, joy, and apprehension as she feels it. Novels are about experiencing other people's lives and problems. Bouncing around dissipates this and weakens the story's impact. By keeping the viewpoint tight, we inevitably also heighten the possibilities of dramatic conflict. It bears repeating here that the reason you should do a synopsis is to figure out *what* the story is. In selecting a POV, you're now figuring out *how best* to tell that story. A description of a place or person will be different if viewed through the hero's eyes or the villain's.

10. *Novels are not straight lines of narrative but circles or spirals that should continually revisit old information in new ways.* This is a bit more than plain foreshadowing, which is also important, but is obviously related. Chekhov said, "If you pull a gun in Act 1, you must fire it in Act 3." Everything in a novel should have a purpose and, if possible, should do "double duty." That is, a piece of information can perform one function on page 10, and then take on a different and equally important function by page 60. The British author Robert Goddard is brilliant in this regard as, too, are some of the better mystery writers. All novels, in some respects, are mysteries in the sense of what we are told, when we are told it, and how we are told it. The technical term is *pacing of information.* Mastering this is one of the major elements of good storytelling. Once the reader grasps that the author is writing in this spiral or circular form, they also realize they can't afford to skip a word, and as a result the novel becomes much more compelling to read.

11. *Avoid exposition of any kind, particularly in dialogue, and also avoid long, internal monologues.* For example, "Oh

Charles, is that you standing in the doorway with a three-fifty-seven turbocharged magnum pistol with hollow-pointed copper bullets?" "Yes, Amanda. And it's pointed right at you." "Oh Charles, I'm so frightened," shuddered Amanda. "So you should be, Amanda," Charles threatened, "for I intend to shoot you with it."

Or, "The dead boy came from Paris," said the inspector. "It's the French capital you know," retorted Jeffrey knowingly. "Do you know the story of Joan of Arc?" asked the inspector. "Yes, but remind me," remarked Jeffrey.

The reason that writing a novel is so difficult is precisely because solving problems of pacing of information and point of view is so hard.

12. *Avoid showing off and dazzling us with your brilliant virtuosity with language.* If we become aware that you, the author, are getting in the way, the novel isn't working and is probably overwritten. It's rather like someone whispering in your ear while you're trying to watch a movie. At the very least, it's distracting. Don't confuse "I" the author with "I" the character in first-person novels. Don't write stories in any other tense than the past unless there's a really good reason. Editors hate it. Avoid phrases that sound great but are literal nonsense or pretentious. Do not comment on the action or characters. For example, "Magdalene threw back her head in a soundless mime of laughter that had been photographed, holographed, silk-screened, reproduced on dinner plates. Showing only the long column of throat. Perfectly phallic, some said. A throat that invited Dracula to fellate it." Remember, *the higher calling is not the writer, but the storyteller.*

13. *Cut everything you can cut, put the novel aside for a week, reread it, and then cut some more.* Find one powerful

descriptive word or phrase to replace the two paragraphs of description (or more) you currently have. Don't repeat yourself. Say it once and move on. Trust the power of language, and don't write defensively.

14. *Keep it simple and direct.* Make sure your work entertains you, because if it doesn't it surely won't entertain anyone else.

15. *Try this exercise:* Write two pages of fiction as badly as you possibly can, using every excess you think you have as a writer and every excess you have noticed in other writers. Then study it, examine your novel, and fix it using this exercise as a guide.

# Appendix B

## Suggested Reading and Reference Books: A Short and Highly Opinionated List

The point of this list is to push ajar a heavy door to a vast domain. I hope something here will lead you to the same delight that all serious writers experience in their discovery of the great writers and thinkers of the world.

The lists are in approximate chronological order of publication so that you get an inkling of how storytelling has developed over the past 1,000 years.

### Nonfiction

*The Tyranny of Words*—Stuart Chase
*The Writer's Handbook* (any edition you can get your hands on)
*The Elements of Style*—Strunk and White
*The Hero with a Thousand Faces*—Joseph Campbell
*Character Analysis*—Wilhelm Reich
*Memories, Dreams, Reflections*—C. G. Jung
*The Art of Fiction*—John Gardner
*On Becoming a Novelist*—John Gardner

On Moral Fiction—John Gardner
The Screenwriter's Workbook—Syd Field
Make Your Words Work—Gary Provost
What If?—Anne Bernays and Pamela Painter
Starting From Scratch—Rita Mae Brown
The Art of Fiction—David Lodge (This has the same title as Gardner's book, and this will no doubt create confusion over time, because both books are excellent, but both tackle their subjects from different perspectives.)
Writing the Blockbuster Novel—Albert Zuckerman

## Useful Reference Books

The Bible
Roget's International Thesaurus
Bartlett's Quotations
Simpson's Contemporary Quotations
Fowler's Modern English Usage
Webster's Collegiate Dictionary, Tenth Edition
The People's Almanac [Vols 1, 2, & 3] (Doubleday/Bantam) These may be hard to find because the last edition was published in 1981.
The Book of Key Facts (Ballantine)
It Was a Very Good Year (Bob Adams)
Any decent up-to-date encyclopedia
Any decent old encyclopedia
Any decent, up-to-date, on-line guide to resources and research on the Internet

## If You Can Afford It

A 28.8 Kbps modem

An on-line membership to Delphi, America Online, CompuServe, or any bulletin board that allows access to digital data sources, either their own or on the Internet.

## Fiction

1300–1400
  *The Canterbury Tales*—Geoffrey Chaucer
1500–1600
  The collected plays of William Shakespeare
1600–1800
  *Pilgrim's Progress*—John Bunyan
  *Paradise Lost* and *Paradise Regained*—John Milton
  *The Life and Strange Surprising Adventure of Robinson Crusoe, of York, Mariner*—Daniel Defoe
  *Travels into Several Remote Nations of the World, by Captain Lemuel Gulliver*—Jonathan Swift
1813
  *Pride and Prejudice*—Jane Austen
1818
  *Frankenstein, or Prometheus Unbound*—Mary Wollstonecraft Shelley
1819
  *Ivanhoe: A Romance*—Sir Walter Scott
1837
  *Twice-Told Tales* and/or *The Scarlet Letter* (1850)— Nathaniel Hawthorne
1840–1850
  The stories of Edgar Allan Poe
1863
  *The Water Babies*—Charles Kingsley
1865–1872
  *Alice's Adventures in Wonderland* and *Through the Looking*

*Glass* —Lewis Carroll
1868
*Little Women*—Louisa May Alcott
1876–1885
*The Adventures of Tom Sawyer* and *The Adventures of Huckleberry Finn*—Mark Twain (Samuel L. Clemens)
Collected stories and essays of Ambrose Bierce
1883–1886
*Treasure Island* and *The Strange Case of Doctor Jekyll and Mr. Hyde*—Robert Louis Stevenson
1885–1887
*She* or *King Solomon's Mines*—H. Rider Haggard
1891
*The Picture of Dorian Gray*—Oscar Wilde
*Tess of the d'Urbervilles*—Thomas Hardy
1892
*The Adventures of Sherlock Holmes*—Sir Arthur Conan Doyle
1895
*The Time Machine: An Invention* and *Goodbye Mr. Chips*—H. G. Wells
*The Red Badge of Courage*—Stephen Crane
1897
*Dracula*—Bram Stoker
1900
*Lord Jim, The Heart of Darkness,* and/or *The Secret Agent*—Joseph Conrad
1902
*Just So Stories, The Jungle Book*—Rudyard Kipling (the first English winner of the Nobel Prize for literature, in 1907)
*The Immoralist*—André Gide
1904
*Cabbages and Kings*—O. Henry (William Sydney Porter)
1908
*The Wind in the Willows*—Kenneth Grahame
1911

*The Secret Garden*—Frances Hodgson Burnett
*Ethan Frome*—Edith Wharton
1912
*Riders of the Purple Sage*—Zane Grey
1913
*Sons and Lovers*—D. H. Lawrence
1914-1916
*A Portrait of the Artist as a Young Man* and *The Dubliners*
—James Joyce
1920
The collected poems of Wilfred Owens (killed in action, 1918)
*The Mysterious Affair at Styles*—Agatha Christie
*The Age of Innocence*—Edith Wharton
1920-1925
*This Side of Paradise* and *The Great Gatsby*—F. Scott Fitzgerald
1926-1952
*The Sun Also Rises, The Old Man and the Sea,* and *For Whom the Bell Tolls*—Ernest Hemingway
1928
*Peter Pan*—J. M. Barrie
1922-1946
*Narcissus and Goldmund, Siddhartha*—Herman Hesse
1928
*Orlando*—Virginia Woolf
1929
*The Dain Curse* and *The Maltese Falcon*—Dashiell Hammett
1930
Collected stories of W. Somerset Maugham
1934
*I Claudius* and *Claudius the God*—Robert Graves
1937-1953
*The Hobbit* and *Lord of the Rings*—J. R. R. Tolkien
1938
*U.S.A.*—John Dos Passos

1939

*The Little Foxes*—Lillian Hellman

*The Grapes of Wrath* and *Of Mice and Men*—John Steinbeck

*The Day of the Locust*—Nathaniel West

1942–1947

*The Stranger* and *The Plague*—Albert Camus

1945

*Down and Out in Paris and London, 1984, Animal Farm, The Road to Wiggan Pier* and other essays and stories—George Orwell (Eric Arthur Blair)

1948

*Cry the Beloved Country*—Alan Paton

1939–1954

*The Lady in the Lake*—Raymond Chandler

1951

*The Catcher in the Rye*—J. D. Salinger

1952

*The Invisible Man*—Ralph Ellison

1952–1963

*The Group*—Mary McCarthy

*Go Tell It on the Mountain*—James Baldwin

*The Illustrated Man, Dandelion Wine,* and *The Martian Chronicles*—Ray Bradbury

1954

*Lord of the Flies*—William Golding

The collected stories, plays, and poems of Dylan Thomas

*I Am Legend*—Richard Matheson

1960

*To Kill a Mockingbird*—Harper Lee

1961

*The Prime of Miss Jean Brodie*—Muriel Spark

*Catch 22*—Joseph Heller

1962

*Briefing for a Descent into Hell, The Fifth Child*—Doris Lessing

*A Clockwork Orange*—Anthony Burgess

1966
> *In Cold Blood*—Truman Capote (Is it a novel or nonfiction? You decide.)

1967
> *The Fixer* and *The Natural*—Bernard Malamud
> *Sophie's Choice* and/or *The Confessions of Nat Turner*—William Styron

1970–Present
> *Heat and Dust*—Ruth Prawer Jhabvala
> *Burr*—Gore Vidal
> *The Spy That Came In from the Cold*, *The Perfect Spy*, John le Carré
> *Grendel*—John Gardner
> *Watership Down*—Richard Adams
> *The Joy Luck Club*—Amy Tan
> *Childhood's End*—Arthur C. Clark
> *Ragtime*—E. L. Doctorow
> *Time After Time*—Jack Finney
> *The Cage*—Michael Weston
> *The Wings of the Wind*—Ronald Hardy
> *The Prince of Tides* and/or *The Great Santini*—Pat Conroy
> *The Color Purple*—Alice Walker
> *Jazz*—Toni Morrison
> *The Chaneysville Incident*—David Bradley
> *Past Caring* and *In Pale Battalions*—Robert Goddard

# About the Author

Peter Rubie, a former BBC Radio and Fleet Street journalist, was the award-winning fiction editor at Walker and Company for nearly six years. He is currently a partner in L. Perkins Associates, literary agents in New York City.

Rubie is the author of two novels, *Mindbender* (Lynx) and *Werewolf* (Longmeadow Press), a dark thriller, as well as the nonfiction *Hispanics in Hollywood* (Garland). He is currently at work on a new thriller, *The Resurrectionist*, which is set in nineteenth-century New York City. He has also written several screenplays, and is often a guest lecturer at universities and writer's conferences. Otherwise, he can sometimes be found popping in to the Time Warner Writer's Conference on CompuServe. Rubie lives and works in New York City and has two cats, Bonkers and Piglet.